Guardian Angels

How To Activate Their Ministry in Your Life

by
Roy Hicks, D.D.

Harrison House
Tulsa, Oklahoma

Unless otherwise indicated, all Scripture quotations are taken from the *King James Version* of the Bible.

Guardian Angels —
How To Activate Their Ministry
in Your Life
Revised Edition
ISBN 0-89274-879-6
Copyright © 1991 by Dr. Roy H. Hicks
P. O. Box 4113
San Marcos, California 92069

Published by Harrison House, Inc.
P. O. Box 35035
Tulsa, Oklahoma 74153

Contents

Foreword

by
Dick Mills

It has been my privilege to read the manuscript for Dr. Roy Hicks' book on angels.

One of the first things I noticed was how many verses in the Bible use the word "angel." It is surprising to find that the Bible is literally full of Scriptures regarding their existence, their names, their function, their presence with us, their ministry and their relationship in the heavens.

While reading the interesting and informative teaching Dr. Hicks has shared with us, I began to ask myself some questions: "Had I ever heard many sermons on the subject of angels? Had I read many books on the subject? Had I ever read poems about them?" I had to answer "no." The pictures painted about them always concern children and their protection. Unconsciously, I found myself remembering the pictures I saw when I was a child but could remember very little information available as an adult.

The subject of angels is not for children only. Dr. Hicks very capably shows that all Christians, regardless of age, can be and should be informed about this most important part of their Christian walk.

It is my firm conviction that before the second coming of our Lord there will be as much angel activity as there was during His first coming.

We owe a debt of appreciation to Dr. Hicks for taking the time out of his busy speaking schedule to gather together this vital information on the subject of angels.

Introduction

For we wrestle not against flesh and blood, but against principalities, against powers, against the rulers of the darkness of this world, against spiritual wickedness in high places.

Ephesians 6:12

These are those invisible evil spirits that are mighty in their warfare against us. But we are not alone in this battle for our spiritual heritage. We have help.

We have the whole armor of God. We have the Captain of the Host, our Lord Jesus, and we have angels, archangels, cherubims, and seraphims.

Satan fell and he, with his deceived angels, were cast out of heaven down to earth. Now we have what we know as evil spirits, demons, principalities, and rulers of this world who fight against us. Most of us who believe all of the teachings of the Bible are for today also believe that we have supernatural help. God has not forsaken us or given us over to accidents or disease. We do not believe the teaching "what is to be will be," or "when it is your time to go, you will go."

So many people have heard for so long that it is God who sends death, destruction and disease that there could be a tendency to think that He also sends sin!

On quite the contrary though, God does not send the above mentioned evils. Rather, He has prepared a mighty host of heaven to assist us. Our problem is that we cannot see with our physical eyes either the good angels or the evil ones. All we see are the results!

That is why Elisha asked God to open his servant's eyes that he might see. When his eyes were opened, he saw **the mountain was full of horses and chariots of fire round about Elisha.** (2 Kings 6:17.)

May God help us to have *open eyes of faith* to know that they that are for us are more than those against us. (2 Kings 6:16.) The Lord, many times, has allowed us to see and know that we have angels assisting us.

A report was smuggled out of Russia that the cosmonauts photographed seven giant figures while orbiting in their space ship, Salyut 7. The Russians will only admit that the photos were enormously revealing but did not believe that Christians could use them to prove their Bible to be true.

We have hundreds of accounts of the activities of angels, some in this book and some in others. Though we enjoy these accounts, we do not propose to need them to prove the reality of angels. God is infinitely more pleased when we accept His Word, believe it, and act upon it.

This book is not full of angel stories, but there are a few. The principle intent of this book is to *stir up your faith in God's Word* and your belief in a personal angel sent to minister to you and for you. (Heb. 1:14.)

Some new thoughts may surface as you read this book. As you read, you can decide for yourself. One new insight will surface that will support the scriptural truth of submission. This teaching may have been abused in times past and caused many of God's people to "throw out the baby with the wash water."

Throughout the book, I trust that I have made it clear that our angels are not completely subservient to us. Though they are sent to minister to us and for us, they cannot ignore our transgressions and sins, and they will not cover them.

Many commentaries teach that it was our Lord Jesus who appeared in the Old Testament instead of angels. The

Bible, as I have said before, is so written that the one reading it will have the freedom to choose what he concludes. So it is with the account of angels. Sometimes they seem to speak and act for themselves. Other times it seems they speak for God.

1

The Angel and Israel

The main purpose of this book is to try and discover what we can about angels and how, and in what way, God uses them to assist us. Above all, we want to be open to any further understanding that can help us to be in a position to receive all God can do through the ministry of angels.

We must be careful to observe, as we read the Bible, that often God used angels, yet man gave honor to God. This is as it should be. People in the Bible, when they had an experience with angelic beings, often said, "The Lord did this." We want to explore, and try to discover if God used angels to bring to pass His will *more often* than we have previously thought he did.

A good place to start is in the book of Exodus, which deals with God delivering Israel from slavery and bondage in the land of Egypt where they had served for 430 years.

God began the great exodus and deliverance by causing Moses to be raised by Pharaoh's daughter. After Moses was grown, he defended one of his Jewish brothers and in so doing, killed an Egyptian then had to flee for his life.

The whole episode of Moses' call and the beginning of the great deliverance started when an angel appeared to Moses (Ex. 3:2 and Acts 7:30) in a flame of fire in the midst of a bush. The bush burned but was not consumed, so Moses drew near to see what he called, **this great sight** (Ex. 3:3).

Now begins a long conversation between God and Moses. When Moses doubted that his brethren would believe him, we read of the miracle of the rod turning into a serpent as Moses threw it to the ground and the miracle of his hand becoming leprous as he thrust it into his bosom.

Whether it was God's voice or God using the angel's voice and speaking in the first person, the Word is very clear throughout its entirety that angels are His messengers. If we come to the conclusion that it was the angel who was speaking for God, it does not take anything away from the Scriptures or the omnipotence of God.

The message is from Heaven. It is Heaven sent, and God is the sender. If it is the voice of God through the angel, that would be all right too, for it would help us to understand more than ever how much God has used His angels to minister His affairs on earth.

God is getting His message across very firmly to Pharaoh. He is going to use His angels to bring it to pass. One difficult portion of Scripture to understand is Exodus 4:24 where the Lord meets Moses and seeks to kill him. Does God do this? Or does this relate to the experience that happened to Balaam when he was out of God's will and an angel met him flashing the sword (2 Peter 2:15,16)? Moses was out of God's will about circumcision.

I do not believe it will do injustice to God or the Scriptures to again believe that God often uses angels to carry out His will here on earth. It is still God's will being done.

Another difficult portion deals with the destruction and death of the firstborn of the Egyptians. Some writers infer that God did it, but Exodus 12:23 (NKJV) reads that God would **not** *allow the destroyer* to kill any of the firstborn of Israel.

You might wonder, ''Why is the Bible written the way it is?'' I believe it is written so men can study it and end up believing what they want to believe (regarding certain issues: some issues are not open for interpretation such as Jesus' dying for our sins and being the only avenue to a restored relationship with God). Some lean toward the teaching of John Calvin and say God kills and destroys. Yet Jesus, in John 10:10, makes it clear that it is the thief, not God, that kills and destroys. Again we read in Hebrews 2:14, **through death he might destroy him that had the power of death, that is, the devil.**

After careful study of the entire Bible, I believe the total teaching of the Word depicts God as the delivering One, not as a destroyer.

Many Bible students believe, as I do, that there was a permissive tense in ancient Hebrew that is not used today. We believe that the Hebrew spoken in Abraham's day was not the same as the Hebrew spoken today. God does *permit* sickness and destruction throughout the Bible.

> **And the angel of God, which went before the camp of Israel, removed and went behind them; and the pillar of cloud went from before their face, and stood behind them: And it came between the camp of the Egyptians and the camp of Israel; and it was a cloud and darkness to them, but it gave light by night to these: so that the one came not near the other all the night.**

> **Exodus 14:19,20**

What a brilliant maneuver by the angel. When he saw the horses of the enemy coming too close to Moses and the people, the angel moved his position from leading them to following behind them in order to protect them from their pursuers.

We must admit that angels are superior to man in every way. They know our needs. They know what to do and where and when to do it. Isaiah 63:9 calls the angel **the angel of His presence** that delivered them.

I have to declare again that I believe that God divided the Red Sea so the children of Israel could go across on dry land. After the people were safely across, He allowed that same sea to drown the Egyptians only after the angels had removed their chariot wheels to slow them down. Exodus 14:31 explains, **And Israel saw that great work which the Lord did upon the Egyptians: and the people feared the Lord, and believed the Lord, and his servant Moses.**

This mighty deliverance by the God of Abraham stands unparalleled in history. The way it was done, and the strategy used was brilliant beyond description. Just think, He did it through His mighty angels, and they stand ready today to help us in our battle against our enemy.

If we can fully accept that God is a delegator and does His work through angels, using them here on earth to work with His saints in mighty deliverance, then we should be open as to what we might be able to do that will open doors so we can receive their assistance!

The battle with Amalek in Exodus 17:3-16 can give us some insight as to what we can do to make ourselves available for the help of angels. When Moses had his hands raised, a type of worship, the enemy was put to flight. When Moses became weary, the enemy prevailed. Then Aaron and Hur, representing the priesthood, gave assistance and joined in helping to hold up Moses' hands. As they did, Israel prevailed and defeated the enemy.

This demonstrates that God uses angels and that true worship brings angelic assistance in our battles. When leadership grows weary in leading the unity of worship, all of the priesthood, the saints, must join in. We are all members of the royal priesthood, a holy nation. (1 Peter 2:5.) Heaven, including angels, comes to our assistance as we worship.

In the midst of God's warnings and commandments, He reminds them that He has given them an angel.

Behold, I send an Angel before thee, to keep thee in the way, and to bring thee into the place which I have prepared. Beware of him, and obey his voice, provoke him not; for he will not pardon your transgressions: for my name is in him.

But if thou shalt indeed obey his voice, and do all that I speak; then I will be an enemy unto thine enemies, and an adversary unto thine adversaries. For mine Angel shall go before thee, and bring thee in unto the Amorites, and the Hittites, and the Perizzites, and the Canaanites, the Hivites, and the Jebusites: and I will cut them off.

Thou shalt not bow down to their gods, nor serve them, nor do after their works: but thou shalt utterly overthrow them, and quite break down their images.

And ye shall serve the Lord your God, and he shall bless thy bread and thy water; and I will take sickness away from the midst of thee. There shall nothing cast their young, nor be barren, in thy land: the number of thy days I will fulfil.

Exodus 23:20-26

Why did God remind Israel and Moses about giving heed to the angel and obeying him? It is possible that God is saying, in effect, "I am a delegator. I assign others to do my bidding. When I do this, it is the same as if I am speaking to you directly." If this is so, and I believe it is, then God is letting us know that we do not have an option when He delegates through an angel.

Even though submission, which is a strong, biblical precept, has been abused in some circles, it must be considered. We are to submit to one another (Eph. 5:21): wives are to submit to their own husbands (Eph. 5:22); the younger are to submit to the elder (1 Peter 5:5); we are to submit to those who have the rule over us. (Heb. 13:17.)

Can you alienate your angel by refusing to be submitted to God's delegated authority? Many pastors can relate lamentable and sad tales of incidents that have happened to people who have caused trouble in the church by their lack of submission.

If God indeed gave us apostles, prophets, evangelists, pastors, and teachers to lead us, then we should submit to that gifted leadership. By not doing so, one can seriously harm one's relationship with the angel that has been assigned to him as an heir of salvation.

If you have ever been involved in any experience, even unwittingly, that has led to the grievous downfall of a man of God or the destroying of a church, please repent and ask forgiveness. The moment you do, the glorious knowledge that you again have the safety of Heaven's protection extended to you in the presence of angels, will flood your heart.

Angel Chronicles

This angel story comes from Church on the Way in Van Nuys, California.

Pastor Jack Hayford related that in the early days of his ministry in Van Nuys he and two of his assistants would go to the church on Saturday nights to pray.

On this particular night, one of the men felt that the Lord wanted each one of them to stand in a corner of the sanctuary and reach out their hands over the seats and worship the Lord.

Since there were only three of them, they had need of one more individual in order to have one in each of the four corners. One of the men recalled that one of the young ladies of the congregation had asked permission to come and pray in the prayer room on Saturday nights. They found her there and asked if she would come and fill the empty corner.

As they worshipped the Lord, the eyes of one of the men were opened in the spirit, and he saw four large angels appear in each corner and stretch forward their wings over the empty seats. When the people wearied and paused, the angels withdrew. When they again worshipped, the angels extended their wings.

This outstanding church has experienced great growth. No doubt they are a worshipping congregation and have the assistance of angels.

2
Angels and Samson

The biblical account of the angel that appeared to the mother of Samson in Judges 13 gives great insight into our study of angels and the important things we need to know about them.

Hebrews 1:14 refers to angels as ministering spirits that are given by God to serve those who believe in Jesus Christ. The Bible states it as a question because, according to Adam Clarke's Commentary, "The Hebrews often express the *strongest affirmative by an interrogation.*" He further states, "They are, no doubt, constantly employed in averting evil and procuring good. If God helps man by man, we need not wonder that He helps man by angels."

Israel once again had failed the Lord, and God's people were under bondage to the enemy. God's plan for the Jews and the coming promised Messiah was being hindered.

God has a plan for His people, but again, He limits Himself to whom He has to work with and not, as some teach, that God can do anything, anytime He wants to.

We would like to discover what seems to affect the angel or his message and his characteristics. Can we discover what pleases or irritates him? In Judges 13, the angel chose to appear to the wife of Manoah, instead of him. Though it would not be true in every case, it does seem to indicate that angels know which one is the most sensitive to spiritual things. In this case, it was Manoah's wife.

---

[1]Adam Clarke, *Commentary on the Holy Bible* (Grand Rapids, Michigan: Baker Book House, 1967), p. 1250.

The angel appeared to Manoah's wife and delivered God's message. He did not say, "Thus saith the Lord." He spoke directly and authoritatively. He had complete knowledge about their marriage, her inability to conceive and even what sex the child would be. He knew about the future because he said the child was to be a Nazarite to God from the womb, and he was to be a mighty deliverer for Israel against the enemy. The angel knew what this would involve for Samson.

Samson was not to drink strong drink of any kind, especially wine. He was not to eat anything unclean, and no razor was ever to be used on his head.

This is excellent information for us to consider as we delve into what the Scriptures teach us concerning angels. It will help us to understand and, if possible, to assist us in securing all of the help and assistance God has made available to us through them.

The angel reveals many of his own characteristics as he delivers his message to Manaoh's wife. He seems to always be aware of the level of our spiritual lives. He did not go to the husband with this important message. Perhaps he did not have the spiritual sensitivity that his wife had. If an angel had a message for you, could he deliver it to you or would he have to give it to someone else?

The angel certainly knew all about humanity concerning physical relationship and the conception of children. This knowledge is important to us in the physical healing ministry and should assist our faith. Whatever was hindering the woman from conceiving is, of necessity, going to have to be healed, or she will not be able to conceive.

We must now try to understand if the angels know the future as God does. If they do, they are more intelligent than the fallen angels, including Satan. Satan, the fallen angel named Lucifer, did not know the future concerning Job's words, **Though he slay me, yet will I trust him** (Job

13:15). If Satan knew Job would say that and not waver, he would never have challenged God about Job.

It seems the angel knew the contents of the sixth chapter of the book of Numbers when he gave the rules for the vow of the Nazarite. Perhaps the reason why he did not go into all of the details, mentioning only wine and unclean food and long hair, is that angels fully expect us to be acquainted with God's Word also. Could this be one of the reasons we do not have more manifestations of the beautiful, awesome creatures? May God forgive us if this is true.

Manoah's wife now comes to him and describes the visit of the angel. She leaves out no details and even adds something to the impression that the angel left on her.

We can expect from her description of him, such as his countenance being different than that of a man, that she knew him to be an angel. Manoah now proves he has great confidence in his wife. He must have believed that his wife was trustworthy. Let all wives take note: you can and may be more sensitive to the spiritual realm than your husband, but do not make the mistake of lording it over him if you want your husband to esteem your spirituality.

Manoah prayed and asked God to let the angel come back and repeat the message. This is a good lesson to all of us. God does not seem to be irritated when we ask His assistance in spiritual understanding unless it is rooted in unbelief, as with Zacharias. (Luke 1:18.)

Manoah did not ask that the angel come to *him*, but to *us*, thus demonstrating that he wanted his wife to be included. Husbands, this is a good thing for all of us to note. Do not exclude your wife, but include her in all of your spiritual exercises. You are to be **one in Him** (Gal. 3:28).

God answered Manoah's prayer and the angel came again to the woman, her husband not being present. She proves again her submission to Manoah by calling for him to both see and hear the angel. This time the angel seems to appear more like a man than before, when he appeared more as an angel. He seems to appear to Manoah to be more like a man because he asked if he was the same one who came before, not knowing yet that he was an angel. Manoah seems to want more ordinary details about Samson and especially his lifestyle and his work.

Then Manoah asks the angel's name. Apparently, angels do not think it is important that we know their names. If there is a time when we need to know, it will be told to us. The only thing he revealed was that his name was secret which may also be translated **wonderful**. (Judg. 13:18 NKJV.)

After this exchange about the name comes one of the greatest lessons we can learn about angels in this story. As Manoah obeyed the angel and offered the sacrifice, a type of worship for us today, a supernatural thing happened. The angel, though he appeared as a man, stepped into the flame of fire and, as they looked on, ascended up toward heaven in the flame.

Here we have a great teaching on the value of sacrificial worship. The angel directed that the sacrifice be offered to God, instead of to him. As they offered the prepared young goat on the flaming altar, the angel used that sacrifice of worship to make his exit back through the earth's atmosphere to heaven.

Do you remember, in the book of Daniel, that the angel, who was bringing back the answer to Daniel's prayer, had great difficulty in getting through the satanic belt that seemed to surround earth? He had to enlist the aid of the mighty angel, Michael, to get the answer through. When Daniel inquired as to why the delay, he was made to understand that the Prince of Persia, who could be an angelic being that rules over Persia for Satan, hindered both the prayer as it went and the answer when it returned. (Dan. 10:13,20.)

What a great truth we learn here about sacrificial worship. It provides a legal right for the angels to ascend and descend to and from God's throne bringing help for the saints.

According to John 4:23, true worship is in spirit and in truth. This goes far beyond, in most cases, what has come to be accepted as worship, the times when we come together as a church body and sing hymns and choruses.

The true worship, the sacrificial worship, is explained to us in Hebrews.

> **By him therefore let us offer the sacrifice of praise to God continually, that is, the fruit of our lips giving thanks to his name. But to do good and to communicate forget not: for with such sacrifices God is well pleased.**
>
> **Hebrews 13:15,16**

Here we have the highest form of worship explained. Notice that the Scripture says to *continually* offer the sacrifice of praise. Thus the sacrifice of praise is not occasional, but continual.

Very few congregations enter into lengthy and sustained periods of worship that call for sacrifice of time and energy. Singing of hymns is good and profitable, but not necessarily sacrificial.

Many churches excel in the enjoyable exercise of singing, clapping, and the joyful dance but fall short in the sacrificial, sustained, pure praise and worship that is devoid of any fleshly manifestation. We need all of the help we can get from heaven. When we worship, we give God a legal right to send help through this Satan-dominated, earthly atmosphere. We need every message God has for us.

Sacrificial, repeated, continuous and sustained worship will furnish the avenue, and God will always do His part.

This kind of worship even goes beyond our coming together in church services. It is meant to be a lifestyle.

Notice Manoah's great fear that his wife did not seem to share. He was afraid that they would die because they had seen God. (Judg. 13:22.) Again, we see why God put man and woman together. We need each other. His wife gives such a simple answer. To paraphrase it, "If God were unhappy, we would be dead already, but God did receive the sacrifice. Thus all is well."

It came to pass as the angel said. Samson was born. During his lifetime, he was mightily used of God to defeat the enemy, and if he had been obedient, he would have perhaps gone down in history as being one of the greatest men in the Old Testament record.

The following are some of the conclusions we may arrive at concerning angels in our study of Judges 13.

1. They seem to have a choice as to whether they will appear to a wife or a husband.

2. They seem to know about barrenness and the birthing of children.

3. They know all about the importance of what the woman eats and drinks while carrying the child in the womb.

4. They seem to be well versed in understanding the Scriptures.

5. They seem to be able, with God, to read future events and understand what is coming to pass.

6. Their countenances at times can be awesome, other times ordinary.

7. They do not like personal questions about themselves or inquiries about their names.

8. God does entertain our requests. In this case, it was a prayer for an angel to return.

9. They seem to be patient and will repeat messages.

10. They do not eat our food.

11. They do not receive worship.

12. Our worship seems to be one of their principal ways of access to (and from) earth.

Angel Chronicles

Chaplain Alex B. Cowie, who has since gone on to be with the Lord, told me this story.

During World War II, he was stationed in the Pacific arena and was riding in a U.S. transport plane when it was attacked by Japanese fighter planes. They were so badly shot up that the pilot said, "We can't make it. We're going down."

As Chaplain Cowie prayed, he looked out the window. The Lord opened his eyes, and he saw a mighty angel holding up the wing of the plane. He looked out the other side and saw another angel holding up that wing.

After they landed, everyone who saw the plane marvelled that they had gotten safely back because it was damaged so badly.

3

Angels in Abraham's Life

Genesis gives us the first recorded appearance of angels as they are sent to do God's work on earth. This first view of these beautiful creatures sets the stage for what and how God uses them throughout the entire Bible. In Genesis 16, we read:

> But Abram said unto Sarai, Behold, thy maid [Hagar] is in thy hand; do to her as it pleaseth thee. And when Sarai dealt hardly with her, she fled from her face.
>
> And the angel of the Lord found her by a fountain of water in the wilderness, by the fountain on the way to Shur. And he said, Hagar, Sarai's maid, whence camest thou? and whither wilt thou go? And she said, I flee from the face of my mistress Sarai.
>
> And the angel of the Lord said unto her, Return to thy mistress, and submit thyself under her hands. And the angel of the Lord said unto her, I will multiply thy seed exceedingly, that it shall not be numbered for multitude.
>
> And the angel of the Lord said to her, Behold, thou art with child, and shalt bear a son, and shalt call his name Ishmael; because the Lord hath heard thy affliction. And he will be a wild man; his hand will be against every man, and every man's hand against him; and he shall dwell in the presence of all his brethren.
>
> And she called the name of the Lord that spake unto her, Thou God seest me: for she said, Have I also here looked after him that seeth Me? Wherefore the

well was called Beer-la-hai-roi; behold, it is between Kadesh and Bered.

Genesis 16:6-14

We will note, from the beginning, that when God needs someone to speak directly for Him to a mortal being, He uses angels. We need to also call your attention to the fact that many times the person, hearing and talking with the angels, uses the name *Lord* in addressing the angelic beings.

Throughout the Bible, the identity of angels has been constantly confused by attributing the words of the angels to God, identifying the speaker by saying, "God said," or "The Lord appeared to me." Do not let this trouble you. Whether it is God or His angel, it is still God directly intervening in the affairs of man to help him know God's perfect will for his life.

The idea of Hagar being given to Abraham to become his wife was Sarah's. She thought she had in Hagar someone who could become a surrogate mother and literally bear a child for her then give it over to her so it could be as her very own child.

But it was then as it is today. Many surrogate mothers have a tendency to change their minds about that child once it is conceived. Sarah, seeing Hagar's attitude change toward her, approaches Abraham. She relates to him that a virtually impossible situation now exists and that he is to get rid of Hagar. Abraham gives his consent for Sarah to discipline her. Sarah's discipline is so harsh that the young Hagar runs away.

God now intervenes and sends one of His angels to bring her a message. You might ask, "Why didn't God just allow her to go her way and disappear?" The angel, sent by God to speak to Hagar, tells her to return and submit herself to Sarah. This action gives us great insight into the compassion of God.

At this point in time, Hagar is the innocent one. It was not her idea to bear a child by Abraham. It was Sarah's. So, literally speaking, God shows Himself quick to act on behalf of the innocent one. If the innocent one will obey God's commands and trust in Him, then God will be quick to vindicate and work in his behalf. We must also remember that this is not an ordinary child inasmuch as Abraham is its father.

It seems that God has obligated Himself to always take care of all heirs connected to the family of faith and promise saying, **They which be of faith are blessed with faithful Abraham** (Gal. 3:9). Even though Sarah seemed to be out of God's perfect will, God is going to cover for that mistake and cause it to work out for the best for Hagar and her unborn son.

May this be a great blessing to you whatever your circumstance may be. Perhaps you have made a mistake, even though your motives were good even as Sarah's were. Believe that God has great love and compassion for you and, if necessary, will send an angel to get you out of the situation you find yourself in at the present time.

The angel gives the order to Hagar to return to her mistress and submit herself. One could ask, ''What could have happened to Hagar if she had not obeyed the angel?'' No doubt, she would have proceeded on her way without an angelic covering and protection, and evil would have befallen her.

Notice how knowledgeable the angels are concerning humanity! He knew she was pregnant and that the child was a boy, so he gave her the name, Ishmael, for the baby. He knew what kind of a man Ishmael would be — a wild man who would fight with everyone he contacted. But even more than this, the angel knew he would die in the presence of his brothers and be at peace with them in the end. (Gen.

25:17,18.) How great is God's foreknowledge! God's angels seem to share in this ability to see into the future also.

Hagar obeys the angel and gives the baby the name, *Ishmael.* The obedience of Hagar does not end with this story, for in Genesis 21:9, after Sarah bears Isaac, there is trouble again. This time it does not seem to be Hagar's fault but Ishmael's. He is about fourteen years of age and is the cause of the trouble.

The apostle Paul records in Galatians 4:22-31 a complete record of what happened. Paraphrasing it, Ishmael laughs and scoffs at Isaac in such a provocative way that it is called persecution by Paul. What the boy did must have caused great pain to all concerned. No doubt, Ishmael was old enough to know that he was not now to be the heir to Abraham's wealth and position. He was not the be number one or even number two. He would be outside looking in from here on.

The problem was so bad that as Isaac grew up, it became an unbearable situation for all concerned. Abraham did not like the idea of sending away his firstborn son. He did seem to love the lad and must have spent much time with him as he grew up, especially before Isaac was born.

Paul the apostle refers to this problem as a type of our new born-again nature and the old nature with its unsaved brain and body. Our old, fallen, fleshly nature is not to inherit the promise. It was born and shaped in iniquity, and it is constantly in warfare with our new nature that seeks to walk in the promises and be spiritual. Just as God told Abraham to send the one born of the flesh away, so are we to expel the old fleshly nature and its desires.

The two boys could never live together in peace and neither will our two natures. We must constantly crucify the flesh and keep that unspiritual part of us under so that we are not destroyed.

We see a very heavy scene as Abraham gives Hagar bread and water and very remorsefully sends her away with Ishmael. He could have made it easier for her by giving her wealth and servants and beasts of burden, but he didn't because he knew in his heart that the separation was to be final. She was not to return with the lad, hence there must be a harsh finality to his act. So must our separation from the flesh be, though sometimes it is painful.

Now we are to learn one of the greatest blessings in our Christian walk. If we will do what God says to do and separate ourselves from the flesh, send it away to die as it were, constantly putting it under, then God will take care of all things and even send an angel, if needed, to assist us as He did for Hagar after she and her son had been cast into the wilderness by Sarah.

> **And God heard the voice of the lad [Ishmael]; and the angel of God called to Hagar out of heaven, and said to her, What aileth thee, Hagar? fear not; for God hath heard the voice of the lad where he is.**
>
> **Arise, lift up the lad, and hold him in thine hand; for I will make him a great nation. And God opened her eyes, and she saw a well of water; and she went, and filled the bottle with water, and gave the lad drink. And God was with the lad; and he grew, and dwelt in the wilderness, and became an archer.**
>
> **Genesis 21:17-20**

Even though Abraham had to do a very painful thing, God rewarded him by personally looking after his first son and providing for him in as much as Abraham could not do so and still be in God's perfect will. When we obey, as Abraham did, God will see to it that our sacrifices made in the flesh will not go unrewarded. When we refuse to enjoy the hedonistic pleasures of this world, God will provide far greater pleasures. When we give sacrificially of our substance, God will send angels to make it up to us.

When we submit ourselves to each other, even though painful it may be, you can expect an angel, if necessary, to see you through and give you an expected end. (Jer. 29:11.) Oh, if saints only knew the gracious rewards of obedience! The call for presenting our bodies a living sacrifice (Rom. 12:1) brings great rewards even to the availability of angels when needed. From the very beginning of the Bible, God makes it very clear that we will have angels at our side when needed, as long as we obey.

As I travel around the country, I hear many questions about angels. While there is some truth that we may command our angels to do our bidding, we do not have clear scriptural reference to state that we can do this anytime and for anything we please. If there were clear instances supported by Scripture, there probably are some people who would take it too far! Can't you just hear someone say, "Now angel, if I decide to take a nap, you keep the car on the road while I sleep!"

One young man could not understand why his angel did not watch over his vehicle when it was broken into and his radio was stolen. I explained that if he was a special missionary, on assignment like Abraham's servant who was sent to bring back a wife for Isaac then he, no doubt, could make the same claim on the ministry of angels.

It is not taught in Scripture that a Christian can command his angel to do anything he desires, whenever he wants. But the Scriptures clearly teach that God will meet our needs and many of our desires that are in His will as we exercise our faith and are obedient to His word.

Angel Chronicles

A Church of Christ pastor had received the Baptism of the Holy Ghost and spoken in tongues. After this, he had to give up his pastorate. He and his wife decided to get away from the phone and other interferences and take a long drive in the country to talk and pray.

They were not paying attention to where they were going and found themselves miles away from the city on a dirt road. There were no houses, not even fences, when suddenly their car stopped running. When he looked for the problem, he discovered the battery cable had burned in two. He had no tools or wire and was contemplating the long walk back to find help.

While the pastor tinkered around with the car, his wife opened her Bible and was reading where the angels of the Lord encamp around those who fear Him. She said, "Lord, I believe this. Now, please send an angel to get us out of this fix."

Minutes after she said this, a pick-up truck came along and the driver said, "Can I help you?" The pastor related how the battery cable had burned in two. The truck driver said, "No problem. I am a garage mechanic, and I am moving from one location to another and have the part you need right here. I can fix it for you." He repaired the damage and then drove away without accepting payment for his work.

To this day, they believe it was an angel, for no one would be moving from one location to another on that little dirt road to nowhere!

4

The Angel and Gideon

Because the earth is under the dominion and rule of Satan (2 Cor. 4:4) and evil angels, God's people are constantly pulled toward evil. If God, in the book of Judges, could have intervened and turned the people's hearts away from evil, then Israel, His people, could have had rest from the enemy for a season. God has chosen to give man a free will; thus He could not intervene. God had to, as He always does, judge and punish evil. If there is sin in your life, repent of it. God loves you, but He hates all sin and all evil and must judge it.

This account in the book of Judges deals with the time when God delivered Israel into the hands and dominion of evil men. It was a time of servitude, almost as cruel as when they were captive in Egypt. Their determination to do evil was in spite of ample warning given by God through His angel in Judges 2.

> And an angel of the Lord came up from Gilgal to Bochim, and said, I made you to go up out of Egypt, and have brought you unto the land which I sware unto your fathers; and I said, I will never break my covenant with you.
>
> And ye shall make no league with the inhabitants of this land; ye shall throw down their altars: but ye have not obeyed my voice: why have ye done this?
>
> Wherefore I also said, I will not drive them out from before you; but they shall be as thorns in your sides, and their gods shall be a snare unto you.

> **And it came to pass, when the angel of the Lord spake these words unto all the children of Israel, that the people lifted up their voice, and wept. And they called the name of that place Bochim** [weeping]: **and they sacrificed there unto the Lord.**
>
> **Judges 2:1-5**

I must speak out here against the doctrine of fatalistic predestination. One reason I do is that this doctrine, practiced and believed in by over ninety percent of Protestant people, points to God as the one responsible for the earthquakes, floods, sicknesses, accidents, deaths, plagues and all other traumatic events that could happen to mankind. The teaching is so pervasive that it has reached outside of the church, and people who are not believers and who suffer tragedies lay the reason for their heartache at God's door.

This doctrine teaches that God is the One who predestinates you to either heaven or hell. If God does not select you, then you cannot go to heaven. It seems to me that to believe that doctrine implies that God is the problem. When I read the Bible and look around me, I see man as the problem, not God.

God is very patient and longsuffering in His dealings with us. Please do not let your faith be shaken when trouble comes your way. We cannot live totally free of trouble as long as we are in a devil's world. Just know that God is a covenant maker and a covenant keeper. Don't dwell on your trouble. Let your mind and thoughts dwell on His deliverance. **Many are the afflictions of the righteous:** *but the Lord delivereth him out of them all* (Ps. 34:19).

In Joshua 23, Joshua is nearing the end of his life. He reminds the nation of Israel that the God they serve is a covenant keeper and will continue to drive out the nations from before them as long as they give heed to the covenant and do not bow down to other Gods.

36

In Judges 6:25, the angel insists that Gideon must destroy the altar to Baal in his community before he, the angel, can use him. God, here, is on record that He does not drive out, rebuke or take authority over the enemy without our obedience. We must do our part! Do not waste your prayer time asking God to do anything about the devil. We are told to take that action ourselves in James 4:7, **Resist the devil, and he will flee from you!**

God instructed Israel in Deuteronomy 28 to obey the Lord (v. 1). If they would, then the enemy would flee before them seven ways (v. 7).

At this time in their history, Israel had fallen into the power of the Midianites, a very harsh and evil enemy, for seven years. It was constant vexation. Not only did the Midianites lord it over them ruthlessly, but they stole their cattle and sheep and used the scorched earth policy to destroy their crops. Then Israel cried out to the Lord. I am sure they must have repented.

The Lord then sends an angel to help them. This pattern in the Bible occurs time after time. When God needs a special assignment accomplished on earth, He sends one of His choice angels. This time the angel comes to a man named Gideon in Judges 6.

Gideon reminds the angel, as if he didn't already know, that he was from the weakest tribe of Israel and, in his own opinion, the least in his father's house. The angel of the Lord must have had great reason for choosing such a humble man. Perhaps here is a great key as to how to activate your angel — be truly humble! True humility is in knowing you can do nothing in yourself. Someone has said that one is truly humble when he feels he is unworthy — but others say of him that he is worthy.

Only as you acknowledge God's grace and forgiveness are you able to serve God well. The apostle Paul, not perceived by many to be humble, always confessed that of all sinners he considered himself to be chief, but he could do all things through Christ who strengthened him.

Gideon was not afraid to test the spirits to find whether or not they were of God. He did this by offering a sacrifice to God before the angel. The angel responded by causing fire to come out of the rock and consume it as a burnt sacrifice to the Lord.

As before, in this book, we are brought to a time of decision. Did God continue to use the angel, or did God take over and converse with Gideon? I believe that as it was in the case with Moses so was it here. Though God continues to use the word *angel*, it is God doing it and that is why the Bible used the two terms interchangeably as though they were one.

Gideon was given directions to tear down the altar that his father had built to Baal. He was instructed to destroy the idol by it and offer some of his father's animals as a sacrifice to the Lord.

God's Word for us today may not be to tear down heathen temples, but it is even more direct. **Love not the world, neither the things that are in the world. If any man love the world, the love of the Father is not in him** (1 John 2:15). We, as Christians, are just as guilty of building altars to our gods. Anything *of* or *in* the world that takes us away from our commitment to God has become an altar to a god other than our Lord. It could be a form of time consuming entertainment: television, movies, boating, fishing, golf, or tennis. It challenges us to be ever on the alert against these diversions that so subtly carry us away from our close relationship with our loving God.

It is impossible for us today to understand how great and awesome was this task. His mission was to destroy the chief sanctuary and tear down the stronghold of Satan. Gideon now risks his father's fury and the threat of Baal's henchmen who sought to kill him. He fully realized the price he might have to pay.

Angels are looking for just such Christians today, people of valor who will have the same courage to stand up, risk their lives, or at least expose themselves to the ridicule of an ungodly world. We can, with the same spirit of Gideon, have a firm testimony against sin and take our stand for God.

Gideon's task was such a fearful thing that he chose nighttime to perform it. We glean from this that God wants us to use wisdom in how we serve Him in our environment, as long as we do not compromise. Gideon obeyed God and destroyed the altar to Baal. One act of great courage in the life of a believer will often trigger courage in another. Gideon's father now stands up to the men of Baal and refuses to give in to their demand that he give his son to them. He even chides them about their god being so weak that they had to defend him. He goes one step further and declares that the person who defends Baal be put to death.

Today, on every hand, good men are on the defensive, building a case for the doctrines they cling to. "Miracles are not for today," some say. Others say, "Tongues are not for today." Some even go so far as to say, "Tongues are of the devil." We hear them say that divine healing is not for today, that it passed away with the original twelve apostles. If these doctrines of denial are so secure in their minds, why do they constantly defend them?

Why is it that some who believe in miracles, divine healing and speaking in tongues, sometimes sound defensive also? We do not have to defend the Bible and our pentecostal doctrines. All we have to do is proclaim them and practice them. God will be the defender of His Word and put to silence those who deny them.

This great act of courage by Gideon caused Joash, his father, to change his son's name to Jerubbaal. May we all be so used of God that people will not think of us as we were once known, but as we are now — one having a new identity, a new name!

This story of Gideon and his obedience to God's commands brought about deliverance to God's people. It is written about in this book so we can better understand how, and why, an angel might select a man from among us to do a great work for God. What does the angel look for? What did he look for in Gideon? As we follow Gideon to his successful battle, we can see time and time again why the angel chose him.

1. He, Gideon, was a truly humble man. He confessed his lack of ability without God and truly knew he was the least in his tribe and in his father's house.

2. He was not afraid to test the angel to be sure he was from God. Our heavenly Father and the angels seem to approve of our caution as long as it is not in unbelief.

3. Gideon was chosen because he was not afraid to follow the angel's orders even though it meant risking his life.

4. He was not afraid to have his volunteer army trimmed down to a very few men in order for God to receive the glory.

5. He was not afraid to use a new method in defeating the enemy, using trumpets and candles within pitchers, believing God for victory with simple, childlike faith.

6. He did not stop until he had completely destroyed the enemy, according to instructions, following them explicitly to do so.

7. He believed in supernatural signs, putting the fleece before God twice for a miracle of confirmation before he faced the enemy.

8. Gideon was a worshipper. (Judg. 7:15.)

9. He put God first and himself last. His priorities were evident in the battle cry he chose, The sword of the Lord, and of Gideon (Judg. 7:18).

10. Above all, he sought not any reward for his obedience, refusing to let them proclaim him king in Israel. (Judg. 8:22,23.)

Although God was extraordinarily glorified through Gideon's obedience in this illustration, the end of the story is not a good one. Gideon was, after all, a mere human being with weaknesses. He failed to establish true worship and instead erected an image made by hands for Israel to worship.

In Gideon's day, the angel needed a person to do God's work. If he is searching today for such a person, may we strive to live that humble life before God so it could be possible that we might be another "Gideon" sent to bring deliverance from the bondage of the enemy to God's people.

Angel Chronicles

Having had the privilege of sitting under the ministry of Aimee Semple McPherson, I have heard her relate many accounts of the ministry of angels. The following is one of them.

She first began her ministry as a young woman on the east coast, using a gospel tent. As she related it, she arrived at a certain city, and the people who assisted her had unknowingly pitched the tent on some property that was used as a place for the local young men to play baseball. She was told this, but it was too late to change plans. They had to go ahead as planned, at least for the first night.

As the service began, she saw the angry young men coming from the bushes around the tent. They were carrying gasoline cans, and she knew they intended to burn the tent.

She relates, "I said to the Lord, 'What shall I do?' " The Lord told her to lift her hands and begin to worship Him. As she obeyed, her eyes were opened in the Spirit, and she saw the tent completely surrounded by a host of angels with their wings extended and touching, wing tip to wing tip. As she opened her eyes, she saw the men, all with looks of astonishment on their faces. They had dropped the cans and stood there with mouths agape. Later on, many of them began to attend the services, and many were saved.

When Angelus Temple, the beautiful church seating 5,300 people which Mrs. McPherson built in Los Angeles, California, was erected, she had the painters stencil angels, wing tip to wing tip, around the perimeter of the auditorium just under the huge dome to commemorate the event.

5
Angels as Messengers

This chapter on the subject of angels is being undertaken in order to examine in what godly manner we need to conduct ourselves to receive their assistance when it is needed while on our earthly pilgrimage.

In the first chapter of Luke, the angel Gabriel appears to the Priest Zacharias with the announcement of the coming birth of their baby, who is to be named John and will later come to be known as John the Baptist. He will be used mightily of God to prepare the way for the ministry of our Lord Jesus, as was prophesied. This account reads as follows:

> There was in the days of Herod, the king of Judea, a certain priest named Zacharias, of the course of Abia: and his wife was of the daughters of Aaron, and her name was Elisabeth. And they were both righteous before God, walking in all the commandments and ordinances of the Lord blameless. And they had no child, because that Elisabeth was barren, and they both were now well stricken in years.
>
> And it came to pass, that while he executed the priest's office before God in the order of his course, according to the custom of the priest's office, his lot was to burn incense when he went into the temple of the Lord. And the whole multitude of the people were praying without at the time of incense.
>
> And there appeared unto him an angel of the Lord, standing on the right side of the altar of incense. And when Zacharias saw him, he was troubled, and fear fell upon him. But the angel said unto him, Fear not,

Zacharias: for thy prayer is heard; and thy wife Elisabeth shall bear thee a son, and thou shalt call his name John. And thou shalt have joy and gladness; and many shall rejoice at his birth. For he shall be great in the sight of the Lord, and shall drink neither wine nor strong drink; and he shall be filled with the Holy Ghost, even from his mother's womb.

And many of the children of Israel shall he turn to the Lord their God. And he shall go before him in the spirit and power of Elias, to turn the hearts of the fathers to the children, and the disobedient to the wisdom of the just; to make ready a people prepared for the Lord.

And Zacharias said unto the angel, Whereby shall I know this? for I am an old man, and my wife well stricken in years.

And the angel answering said unto him, I am Gabriel, that stand in the presence of God; and am sent to speak unto thee, and to shew thee these glad tidings. And behold, thou shalt be dumb, and not able to speak, until the day that these things shall be performed, because thou believest not my words, which shall be fulfilled in their season.

And the people waited for Zacharias, and marveled that he tarried so long in the temple. And when he came out, he could not speak unto them: and they perceived that he had seen a vision in the temple: for he beckoned unto them, and remained speechless.

And it came to pass, that, as soon as the days of his ministration were accomplished, he departed to his own house. And after those days his wife Elisabeth conceived.

Luke 1:5-24

This heavenly appearance was the breaking of a great spiritual silence that had hovered over Israel for over 400 years. Something of great significance was about to break forth. God was going to use His heavenly created beings to help with His work on earth.

A God Who is sovereign in His own kingdom, can do what He wills only when He has the cooperation of His people. This He must have. In this situation, He sends one of His mighty angels to begin the final act of the great story and plan of salvation. Subsequently, Jesus will be born and will die for the human race. Man will now have a choice. God's will and purpose on earth is dependent upon finding people of obedience who will believe.

The Jews were raised up and gathered back to Palestine for the unfolding of God's great plan that is now to be finalized. Zacharias, a high priest from one of the sacerdotal families, is in the right place at the right time. He is in Jerusalem, in the temple, in the right time in history. Both he and his wife, though elderly, are to be used. God will leave no doubt that the plan of salvation is to be supernatural all the way from beginning to end. Just as God waited until Sarah and Abraham were well past the time of conception, again He has waited so that there will be no doubt as to who is in charge and who planned the glorious outcome.

It must be noted that Elisabeth and Zacharias were both righteous and blameless before the Lord. To be found blameless before the Lord implies that they had not allowed what many had construed as an unanswered prayer to cause them to become bitter. If they had, they would not be called blameless before the Lord.

There are many of God's finest people who allow themselves to become discouraged and defeated over their disappointments, especially if they feel God has failed them.

If you have been guilty, please repent quickly and once again become available before God for His mighty acts and answers to your prayers. *Angels are not sent to minister to bitter saints.*

Zacharias continues to go about his great calling and ministry. He did not, even in his old age, sit around and complain about being childless. He was ministering praise, through the burning incense before the Lord, when the beginning of that answer to his lifelong request began.

We can learn a great lesson here. Continue to worship and praise God, regardless of all the seemingly negative situations and circumstances. Do not give in to your feelings. Always do and say what you believe God can do about your situation, and you will experience heaven's assistance.

You might think, "Zacharias had a great advantage being in the temple of God, but I am unable to do that." According to 1 Corinthians 3:16, you are the temple of God! You can offer beautiful worship and praise, which is as incense before the Lord, anytime you desire.

You might say, "If only I could get to Jerusalem, as was Zacharias, I might find help." Jerusalem, according to Isaiah 2:3, is where the Word of God flows forth. Our Jerusalem can be our tongue, as it were, where the Word of God issues forth day and night.

If you are tempted to counter, "But Zacharias was one of the chosen priests of God," then I would ask you to read 1 Peter 2:5 which says, **Ye also, as lively stones, are built up a spiritual house, an holy priesthood, to offer up spiritual sacrifices, acceptable to God by Jesus Christ.** In other words, you are just as much a priest unto God as was Zacharias.

The angel Gabriel appears to Zacharias and delivers a message saying that he and his wife are to be blessed with the answer to their lifelong prayer. Do not ever give up. Your answer will come. Continue to offer praise and worship to God. Even when it seems God has waited too long and all physical circumstances are against you, believe and keep on believing.

After Zacharias hears the great news that was delivered supernaturally by Gabriel in great detail, he, like so many of us, allowed unbelief to take over, and he doubted God.

He now begins to allow unbelief to flow from his brain to his lips, as he reminds the angel how old he and Elisabeth are. He must have implied that surely Gabriel, being an angel, must know that people in their eighties do not have children.

It would be appropriate here to remind ourselves of the story of Abraham and Sarah, one that certainly Zacharias should have remembered. If God had done it once, He certainly could do it again.

But before we judge him too harshly, are we not all guilty of allowing our tongue to speak of the impossible first, instead of the possible? So very quickly we speak of earthly barriers before we speak of heavenly power and possibilities. Say *first* what you believe God can do and not how impossible the situation looks!

Now we arrive at a very important place in this great story. The angel Gabriel, in this case, seems to be able to act on his own, as also do other angels when doubt and unbelief are spoken aloud. Let us consider what his options are.

He can leave and go back to God and report this as a failure because of the unbelief he encountered. He can punish the unbeliever on the spot. Even better, he can shut off the very source of unbelief so God's will can be done on earth as it is in heaven. He chooses the last of his options and takes away the ability of the priest to speak.

Because the angel chose to make Zacharias dumb, we can conclude that unbelief in the brain will not get into the heart if it does not pass through the mouth! This principle is so important I wish you would read it again.

The angel Gabriel summarizes to Zacharias, saying that he, Gabriel, who stands in the presence of God, had brought good news, and it is received with a confession of doubt and unbelief.

Oh, that we would learn from this great account. There can be no supernatural help from heaven, from the presence of God, when we insist on speaking of things as they are. We must remember, as Abraham did, that we serve a God Who **calls things that are** *not* **as though they** *were* (Rom. 4:17 NIV) and not a God that calls things that are, as though they were not. Abraham never did say, "Sarah and I are too old," but instead he praised God and gave Him glory for what He *could* do.

Do not discuss your ailment or its symptoms as they are. Instead, talk about the faithfulness of God to watch over His Word and perform it and what a great Healer He is now, today. You do not talk about what great sinners your loved ones are. When you speak of them, you speak of what you believe they will become — people saved by the grace of God, loving Him with all of their hearts.

Do not talk negatively about your children's spiritual condition, especially in front of them. Talk about them by faith, how you believe they will be, serving God and part of His great family. We too, even as Zacharias, can turn our angel off by saying the wrong thing in his presence.

> **Suffer not thy mouth to cause thy flesh to sin; neither say thou before the angel, that it was an error: wherefore should God be angry at thy voice, and destroy the work of thine hands?**
>
> **Ecclesiastes 5:6**

Zacharias almost blew it, and if the angel had not acted quickly to stop his negative tongue, we would not have this story in the Bible. Someone else would have been chosen.

I wonder how many people who God called reacted like Zacharias did? Are there many that we have never heard of in church history because their negative tongues spoke out in unbelief from their brain, instead of from their believing hearts?

Zacharias was unable to talk for many months and could only speak, and apparently hear again, when the child, John, was born. He wrote out on a tablet, **His name is John** (Luke 1:62,63). Then he could speak and praise God and give the great prophecy about things to come.

What a great comparison we have when we consider this same great angel's announcement to Mary, a saint who served God as well. She did not speak unbelief. She did not say, "This cannot be because I have not a husband." Her response was one of curiosity, rather than a lack of faith.

It seems that neither God, nor angels, resent us asking questions. Not only do they not resist our questioning, but they are rather quick to respond with an explanation.

The angel Gabriel ends this glorious announcement to Mary by making one of the greatest statements in our Bible using the Greek word *rhema*. In Luke 1:37, she says, **For with God nothing shall be impossible.** The *American Standard Version* states, **For no word [rhema] of God shall be void of power.** *The Amplified Bible* says, **For with God nothing is ever impossible, and no word from God shall be without power or impossible of fulfillment.** Mary simply said, "No *rhema* from God is devoid of power." In other words, what God says is *possible*, but we must say it exactly as He says it.

We must believe in our hearts, but we must be careful to avoid the interfering thoughts that come from the brain, which are usually thoughts of doubt and fear. Remember that our bodies, of which the brain is a part, are not saved yet. They will be redeemed further down the eschatological road. At this point, all parts of our bodies have no life, except what comes by, and because of, impulses from the brain.

Recently, it has been determined in the courts of law that to be *legally dead* one must be declared to be *brain dead*.

The physical body has no power to move unless it receives direction from the brain. This is illustrated by occasions when an individual has a limb amputated. When that limb is severed from the body and laid aside, it does not have the ability to hop across the room. It has been severed from the brain which controlled it. This illustrates to us that it is the *brain*, not merely the *flesh* alone, that is the real culprit. One of our most difficult, never ending aspects of spiritual warfare is in constantly *resisting* the negative words and constantly *affirming* what God says about our condition!

Mary said, **Behold the handmaid** [slave] **of the Lord; be it unto me according to thy word** [rhema] (Luke 1:38). She did not go away saying negative things, but her faith was active. Not only did she speak positively, but she went to visit Elizabeth and share with her the fulfillment of the *rhemas* of God.

Please do not allow Satan to come and steal this precious seed. Believe, and continue to believe, that angels are God's messengers. Continue to believe that no word, *rhema*, of God is void of power. Know that, though you believe the Word of God, if your tongue contradicts it, you will miss God's promise. Do not speak from your unsaved brain but say only what you believe with your heart.

Angels seem to be very sensitive to our words. Words do not seem to be only related to the temporal realm, but also to the eternal realm. Jesus taught that we are to be redeemed and justified, or condemned, by them.

Spiritually sensitive people can discern an atmosphere created by words of doubt and unbelief. *Cultivating a discipline of our conversation is a spiritual essential if we are going to have the victories that come from saying what God says about every situation.*

After studying the angel's interaction with both Zacharias and Mary, we can conclude the following:

1. Angels do not seem to assist saints who have become bitter.

2. The temple was the place for the Word and worship. We are the temple. (1 Cor. 6:19). Angels seem to honor worship, both private and corporate.

3. Zacharias was a priest, and so are you. (1 Peter 2:5.)

4. Zacharias and Elisabeth had prayed many years for a child, and God answered their prayer. Never give up. Keep believing.

5. Do not allow unbelieving thoughts in your brain to become words in your mouth.

6. Say first what you believe God can do and not how impossible the situation looks.

7. Do not say the wrong thing before your angel. Angels listen.

8. Angels do not seem to reject sound questioning.

9. Angels seem to be more sensitive to our words than our actions.

Angel Chronicles

A pastor shared with me a story about an elderly saint who had been to the mid-week prayer service in her church and had returned home rather late in the evening. Just as she turned on the lights, she heard a knock at the door. Unsuspectingly, she opened the door, and there stood a man with an iron pipe in his hand. He moved menacingly toward her with the pipe raised as though to strike her.

Suddenly, he stopped, his eyes widened and his mouth dropped open. A look of great fear came on his face as he seemed to be looking at something behind her. He dropped the pipe and ran down off the porch into the blackness of the night.

She called the police and related what had happened. They believed her story because, not only was her description correct of a man they had already been looking for, but the piece of iron pipe lay there on the porch where he had dropped it.

She believes, and so do I, that the man saw her angel standing behind her.

6

Guardian Angels

At the same time came the disciples unto Jesus, saying, Who is the greatest in the kingdom of heaven? And Jesus called a little child unto him, and set him in the midst of them, and said, Verily, I say unto you, Except ye be converted, and become as little children, ye shall not enter into the kingdom of heaven. Whosoever therefore shall humble himself as this little child, the same is greatest in the kingdom of heaven. And whoso shall receive one such little child in my name receiveth me.

Matthew 18:1-5

Take heed that ye despise not one of these little ones; for I say to you, That in heaven their angels always behold the face of My Father which is in heaven.

Matthew 18:10

In all their affliction he was afflicted, and the angel of his presence saved them: in his love and in his pity he redeemed them; and he bare them, and carried them all the days of old.

Isaiah 63:9

Guardian angels have always been accepted by not only the church, but by most people of all faiths. That our Lord Jesus not only took the time to bless children, even holding some of them in His arms, is ample proof of God's attitude towards the small, helpless ones.

Inasmuch as this is a book whose main purpose is to call our attention to what *activates* and *deactivates* the ministry of our guardian angels to us, we must give space to the words of our Lord Jesus as they relate to the guardian angels.

The question often arises, "If babies have been assigned angels to guard them, why have there been so many maimed, scarred and suffering babies and children? Many have even died. Do some have inept angels? Were some angels, by circumstances, driven to a point where they had to turn their back on families by the disobedience of the parents?"

In Ephesians 6:1-4 and Colossians 3:20,21, we have good, clear teaching and also some commands about parents and children. First of all, if children do obey their parents, they have been promised long life on this earth. If they disobey and fall away from these promises and their covering then they are in great jeopardy. Many do die prematurely, but not all, for the Father sees, looking ahead, that they will repent and return to the way in which they were brought up. Romans 8:29 says, **For whom He did foreknow, he also did predestinate to be conformed to the image of his Son.**

Now parents, hear this warning, **And, ye fathers, provoke not your children to wrath: but bring them up in the nurture and admonition of the Lord** (Eph. 6:4). How do we provoke our children? How do provoked children react? We provoke them by our outbursts of uncontrolled anger. We punish them when they do not deserve it and fail to punish them when they do. We often take our own frustrations out on them.

We live lives with double standards. We sometimes impose on them the rules and limitations that our parents placed on us without examining them to see if they still apply today! We fail to take into account the peer pressures they are under because some of us never had to face the same kinds of stressful situations that they are facing.

Our children then react as the immature, inexperienced children they are! We should only correct in love, never out of frustration and anger or out of our own insecurities.

Angels cannot overcome and do a good job for us and our children if we, as parents, fail to adhere to God's Word. Angels are not going to close doors we so carelessly leave open. Angels are not going to clean germs from our unkept houses. Angels are not going to sit by your swimming pool to guard your little one from falling in. If we insist on driving carelessly, angels cannot do their work of protection. Angels cannot protect a child from wandering away if parents become too involved in their own interests. On and on, these tragic circumstances that come to our attention record our carelessness and the result of it.

When Jesus gave His warning concerning children and their angels, He said that their angels, being in heaven, always behold the face of the Father. (Matt. 18:10.) Even if the guardian angel is assigned to your child to protect it, he cannot act on his own, but only as he receives orders from the Father. So, no matter what the danger might be, the angel can only act as he receives orders from the Father, Who is also responding to the lifestyle and commitment of the parents.

First Kings 14 gives the account of how God reacted to a very wicked king named Jeroboam. He caused the people of God to turn to evil. He made golden calves for them to worship and appointed priests of the lowest nature who were not of the priestly tribe of Levi.

God did all He could do by sending a prophet with power to show signs and wonders to warn them, but it was to no avail. When a son was born to this wicked king and became sick unto death, God did not spare him but allowed him to die; thus, he escaped the evil of his father's house. The child was the only one spared and not judged with the wicked parents. This story is helpful in understanding God's compassion for innocent children.

A difficult question arises as to whether or not the children of the heathen will be in heaven, or will it just be the children of the saved parents who were under one of the covenants, either Old Testament or New Testament? While there is not enough evidence to arrive at a dogmatic conclusion, one can form an opinion. Here are some facts to consider.

When the Jews in Jesus' day cried, **His blood be on us and on our children** (Matt. 27:25), God allowed that to stand, even to this present day, upon the descendants of those who made the statement.

I do not believe that innocent children will suffer in hell, as adults will. What will happen, we do not know. Paul made it clear that the children of the unbelievers were unclean; thus, they were not under a salvation covenant. (1 Cor. 7:14.) There is enough biblical evidence to cause unsaved parents to be very concerned for their children who may be considered unclean or unsanctified because of their own unsaved state.

When Jesus said, **Take heed that ye despise not one of these little ones** (Matt. 18:10), He is referring to all children of the kingdom inasmuch as all of us in the kingdom are to become as little children. If we fail to become as little children in trust and simplicity then we forfeit the protection of our angels. Angels are not merely assigned to children, but to all who shall be heirs of salvation. (Heb. 1:14.)

Is everyone in the kingdom protected? Are all who are saved and continue in simplicity and trust, protected? The latter is certainly taught by Jesus.

Many people who begin their walk with Jesus as little children, who are innocent, sweet, loving and kind, slowly begin to get their eyes on people and gradually begin to emulate their weaknesses and faults instead of the life of Jesus. As they begin to criticize, find fault, gossip, miss church services, stop tithing, become involved in church troubles, then they are no longer acting as children of the kingdom and are no longer under the promises made to the children of the kingdom. This would include the promise of angelic protection.

If only saints would become as little children in trust and simplicity, then the Ninety-first Psalm would cover them. God could protect them. The angels could minister, and terrible, regrettable things would not happen so often.

Not only is the one who no longer conducts himself as a trusting child in jeopardy, but if in his rebellion, he influences a little one to sin or fall, **it would be better for him to have a large millstone hung around his neck and to be drowned in the depths of the sea** (Matt. 18:6 NIV).

Oh, saints, pity you who are no longer sweet, kind, generous, and teachable. Please return to your first, child-like faith and love. It is better to leave a church than to become involved in a split that causes little newborn babes to backslide or become discouraged.

We do not lose our will when we receive Jesus. The will to do either right or wrong remains. We must, by our will, determine to persevere in our desire to cling to the Lord.

Pastors, your people need to hear the balance of grace and holiness that this chapter covers. They need to hear what happens in heaven and what happens on earth because of disobedience.

Your angel can be thwarted from lifting his hand to help you. Obey, obey, obey! Keep a smile on your Father's face as well as on the face of your angel. Work to keep your first love and stay as trusting as a child.

Angel Chronicles

This angel story comes from one of our missionaries who labored for the Lord in the country of Panama.

He and another missionary had gone far back into the interior where the gospel had not been taken before and where there would be fierce persecution. They had a measure of success and started a church from the meeting.

When they returned the following year to minister, one of the new converts pointed to a house in the distance and said, ''Do you remember when you came last year and slept in that house over there?'' They answered in the affirmative. He went on to say that he and some other men were going to kill them while they slept, but they could not because there were two very large men guarding the house while they slept!

The missionary gives praise to God for the protection of angels!

7

Angels and Submission

The apostle Paul, in writing to the churches, was very careful to set in order church government and authority in the home.

He gives headship to the man but requires in that leadership role that the man love his wife as Christ loved the Church and gave Himself for it. (Eph. 5:25.)

Inasmuch as entire books have been written on this subject, I will here treat a phase of this important subject that, heretofore, has had little attention. We want to talk about the ministry of angels as it has to do with the submission of the wife to her husband and also as it has to do with her activity in the church.

> **But I want you to know and realize that Christ is the head of every man, the head of a woman is her husband, and the Head of Christ is God. Any man who prays or prophesies — that is, teaches, refutes, reproves, admonishes and comforts — with his head covered dishonors his Head (Christ).**
>
> **And any woman who [publicly] prays or prophesies (teaches, refutes, reproves, admonishes or comforts) when she is bareheaded dishonors her head (her husband); it is the same as [if her head were] shaved.**
>
> **1 Corinthians 11:3-5 AMP**

First Corinthians 11:3-5 makes it very clear that the New Testament teaches that a woman is allowed ministry in the church on the same level as man. She has the same right to pray or prophesy as he does. It further states that man

59

is not to prophesy, teach or pray with his head uncovered and that a woman is not to do any of these things without her head covered. It further teaches that if a man disobeys in this, he dishonors God. If a woman disobeys in this, she dishonors her head which is her husband.

In the early church, for a woman to refuse to be covered with a veil, a symbol of submission, it was considered that she may as well go ahead and have her head shaved. At that time, it was understood by all that she was not only in rebellion to her husband but now put herself in the position of being thought of as a prostitute. She was now revolting even against God's laws.

On the other side of the marital coin, if a man wore long hair, as the woman did, he likewise showed he was no longer submitted to authority.

> **Does not (experience, common sense, reason and) the native sense of propriety itself teach you that for a man to wear long hair is a dishonor (humiliating and degrading) to him, but if a woman has long hair, it is her ornament and glory? For her hair is given to her for a covering.**
>
> **1 Corinthians 11:14,15 AMP**

We saw great evidence of this during the Vietnam war era. The many young people who dropped out and became known as the hippies of that generation, chose a lifestyle that expressed rebellion against anything that was conventional. One of the first obvious signs of this were the young men who allowed their hair to grow long and unkempt. It was a sign of their rebellion against the establishment, government and sometimes parents.

It is interesting to note here, and gives much cause for praise, that one of the greatest revivals to ever touch our nation came through this generation of young people who were, in reality, searching for the knowledge of God. Literally, tens of thousands of these young people filled our churches and have, since then, matured and become great assets to God's kingdom and our nation.

The apostle Paul is very fair, not just teaching submission of the woman to the man, but equally teaching man's responsibility to the woman. He lays down very strong rules for both, especially as they relate to functioning in public worship.

Submission is not a new doctrine. It is taught clearly in Scripture. Paul not only taught it, but also Peter.

> **Likewise ye younger, submit yourselves unto the elder. Yea, all of you be subject one to another, and be clothed with humility; for God resisteth the proud, and giveth grace to the humble.**
>
> **1 Peter 5:5**

What happens if God's rules for submission are broken? What are the consequences? First Timothy 5:1-15 teaches that when younger widows were no longer submitted to church leadership, they would be in danger of turning to follow Satan.

Is that what Paul is referring to in the text of this chapter that mentions angels in relation to the lack of obedience to the rules of submission that were written for the good of the church?

The writings of twenty-five Bible commentators all seem to agree on the points which follow:

1. All are unanimous that the covering, or veil, was a sign of a woman's submission to her husband.

2. All seem to agree that this submission was not to place them under domination, but it was a security, giving her rights and liberty.

3. All seemed to agree that the lack of submission would affect the ministry of both good and evil angels (the angels that fell with Satan — Rev. 12:9) on her behalf.

4. Some agreed that, if there is rebellion against this submission, good angels draw back and evil spirits move in.

5. Most all agree that there is a hidden intent that takes one back to the rebellion in the Garden of Eden when Eve followed Satan's suggestion, rather than obeying God's Word.

6. Angels are present in the church, especially during the worship time.

7. Some suggest that good angels leave, rather than be exposed to evil of any kind in the church.

8. One commentator, in a book now out of print, interpreted 1 Corinthians 11:10, ". . . for this cause ought the woman to have power *(a veil)* upon her head because of the *(evil)* angels, *(she being tempted by the prince of them to do that which is perpetual cause of shame to her, and which increased her subjection to the man . . . .)*"[1]

9. Other commentators also add, "because of the evil angels."[2]

Here are some facts that we must face. Paul did refer to angels in relationship to the ministry of woman. The fact is clear that women can minister publicly as long as they are submitted to their husband or the covering of a church. If the rebellion of the woman in her ministry in the church took place, it would somehow affect angels as it relates to her behavior.

If such acts of rebellion would lead to the exposure to the devil that is written of in 1 Timothy 5:15, **For some are**

---

[1]Patrick, Lowth, Arnald, Whitby, and Lowman, *A Critical Commentary and Paraphrase on the Old and New Testament and the Apocrypha* (London, 1822).

[2]Matthew Henry, *Matthew Henry's Commentary on the Whole Bible.* Vol. 6 (Old Tappan, New Jersey: Fleming H. Revell, 1935), p. 562.

already turned aside after Satan then the fact of this text must be recognized and dealt with.

Another fact that cannot be ignored is that when women rebelled from their covering, the church or their husbands, many false cults sprang up as a result of this breaking of God's law.

If we can scripturally apply this act of the consequences of rebellion to the woman leaving her covering then we must apply, equally, the same rules to the husband. In Christ, the New Testament and the new covenant, there is neither male nor female. (Gal. 3:28.)

History records many cults following the breaking of submission one to another. The question ought to be asked by every person now caught in what we recognize as false religions or cults: Did this leader break away from his covering? Did he get led away into a new doctrine that differs from the pure doctrine of Scripture? Did he say, "I have a new revelation, follow me?"

Let us scrutinize the break-up of a marriage and a home. If it has deteriorated to where adultery has entered the picture, there are questions to be asked: "When did the immoral thoughts first come? Could it have happened when a wife was in complete submission to a loving husband?" I think not! Just as Eve might not have fallen to Satan's suggestion if she had first consulted with Adam, so would a married couple be able to recognize what was happening, humble themselves and repair the breach. Marriages and homes that are without God stand little chance of survival.

This book is about angels and their faithful ministry to the heirs of salvation. This particular subject is about the withdrawing of their presence and aid when God's laws are broken by the ones they are assigned to help.

In Psalm 78:37-39,41-64 and Exodus 23:23, Israel's angel was faithful to lead and protect Israel until they provoked the Lord God in the wilderness. He then forsook the tabernacle and delivered them into the hands of their enemy. It is very possible for us to turn our angel off just as easily.

Ecclesiastes warns us,

> **Suffer not thy mouth to cause thy flesh to sin; neither say thou before the angel, that it was an error: wherefore should God be angry at thy voice, and destroy the work of thine hands?**
>
> **Ecclesiastes 5:6**

If our angel is provoked into leaving us, we are no longer under their protection. We are now exposed to every evil spirit and have no angelic protection from accidents, diseases, and plagues.

Do everything you can to stay submitted to your husbands. Husbands, do all you can to love your wife as yourself. Do not risk living in a sin-blighted world without angelic protection.

God would say the same thing to us that He said to His people Israel.

> **Behold, I send an Angel before thee, to keep thee in the way, and to bring thee into the place which I have prepared. Beware of him, and obey his voice, provoke him not; for he will not pardon your transgressions: for my name is in him.**
>
> **But if thou shalt indeed obey his voice, and do all that I speak; then I will be an enemy unto thine enemies, and an adversary unto thine adversaries.**
>
> **Exodus 23:20-23**

If you provoke your angel, then God can no longer be an enemy to your enemies or an adversary to your adversaries. In other words, you will have to fight your enemies by yourself, without any heavenly assistance.

Great churches and ministries have been known to literally disintegrate and fall apart. In some cases, it was the wife who strayed from the truth, sometimes the pastor.

At a point when either one, or both, were not submitted to God's order of submission, evil spirits literally moved in and destroyed the church and ministry. Thank God, by His grace, some have turned to Him and sought His help and restoration has come.

May we ever be willing to humble ourselves and go with God's divine order. The price one pays for revolt is never worth the temporary pleasure!

I would like to encourage women that, in Christ, there is neither male or female. They, along with men, can be anointed to minister. The apostle Paul did not mean in 1 Timothy 2:12 that women could not do any public teaching. If he meant that, then he would have contradicted himself in 1 Corinthians 11:5 which states that a woman can be prophesying but must have her head covered to indicate she was in submission. This head covering could also be interpreted as a spiritual covering. A true reading of 1 Timothy 2:12 is, "I will not suffer a woman, teaching, to usurp authority over the man."[3]

In Greek, *didaske* or "to teach" is an infinitive in the present tense which refers to a continuous or repeated action. In other words, it means "to teach continuously." G. Campbell Morgan, in a book out of print, confirms the right of the woman to be teaching.

A woman, in Christ, has the same privilege to minister in both prophesying and teaching as long as she does not usurp authority over the man.

Angel Chronicles

A lady missionary was traveling in a Communistic country, one that suppressed religious freedom. She, following God's word to her, found herself in a small town.

---

[3]Spiros Zodhiates, *Hebrew and Greek Key Study Bible* (Iowa Falls, Iowa: World Bible Publishers, 1984), p. 1474.

She did not know where to go and ended up in a small, dark, dimly lit building. A nicely dressed man walked up to her and said, "You are in the wrong place, aren't you?" She answered and said, "Yes, I believe I am." He told her to follow him, and he led her to a larger building off the beaten path. As they entered and their eyes became accustomed to the dark, she saw over three hundred Christian believers gathered there. They said to her, "God told us to come here today and that He would send someone from America to speak to us."

The lady missionary could not speak their language, but the man could, and he interpreted for her. There is not the slightest doubt that the man was an angel and knew where God had told them to come because, in that nation, you cannot advertise your meeting place.

8

Angels Thwarted

Are they not all ministering spirits, sent forth to minister for them who shall be heirs of salvation?

Hebrews 1:14

The angel of the Lord encampeth round about them that fear him, and delivereth them.

Psalm 34:7

But after long abstinence Paul stood forth in the midst of them, and said, Sirs, ye should have hearkened unto me, and not have loosed from Crete, and to have gained this harm and loss. And now I exhort you to be of good cheer: for there shall be no loss of any man's life among you, but of the ship.

For there stood by me this night the angel of God, whose I am, and whom I serve, saying, Fear not, Paul; thou must be brought before Caesar: and lo, God hath given thee all them that sail with thee. Wherefore, sirs, be of good cheer: for I believe God, that it shall be even as it was told me.

Acts 27:21-25

There shall no evil befall thee, neither shall any plague come nigh thy dwelling. For he shall give his angels charge over thee, to keep thee in all thy ways. They shall bear thee up in their hands, lest thou dash thy foot against a stone. Thou shalt tread upon the lion and adder: the young lion and the dragon shalt thou trample under feet.

Psalm 91:10-13

One of the chapters in this book deals with guardian angels that are assigned to us at birth. For some reason or other, most of us have believed and accepted as fact that angels do watch over babies and children but, in our traditional theology, we have not brought over the doctrine of the ministry of angels into adulthood, at least in discussion or writings. This we must do in order to be 100 percent scripturally minded and correct in theological thinking.

The Scriptures at the beginning of this chapter certainly bear witness to this great truth. Angels are not temporarily assigned to us as children and then abruptly taken away as we become adults! There are too many accounts in the Bible of saints being protected, ministered to, taught and corrected by these beautiful beings. Not only do the angels encamp around about those that fear Him, but they are assigned to keep us and bear us up. (Ps. 91.) With this added assistance we can have the ability to walk all over the enemy!

Does this account of God's promises describe the experience of the average saint in our churches today? The answer is an emphatic, no!

Saints are sickly, die prematurely, are involved in tragic accidents and suffer the devilish destruction of families and homes. Our hearts are made heavy many times because of the things that befall wonderful Christian people. There seems to be no end to the examples of sorrow and confusion found in the lives of men and women who serve the Lord. Surely, God can give us the answer as to why this happens so frequently! The Bible is always forthright and faithful to tell both sides of the story.

Certainly, the covenant families of Abraham, Isaac, Jacob and even Lot were wonderfully ministered to by the angels of the Lord. But some were not able to receive the ministry of angels. Even though we do not have a specific account of angelic intervention in Abraham's life, we do know he had some experience with them and knew of their help. Thus, in relating messages from God he had

68

confidence, or he would have never said to his servant in Genesis 24:7, **he shall send his angel before thee, and thou shalt take a wife unto my son from thence.**

Abraham was old and feared that his son, Isaac, would take a wife from among the heathen. He knew that in order for the blood line of the Messiah to be pure, the right wife for his son must be chosen. He also knew he could depend on the angel for this to come to pass according to God's will, and eventually, Isaac was married to a woman of faith and trust.

Jacob's encounter was of a different nature. Jacob was, in the opinion of many, a cheat and conniver. He faced the wrath of his brother, Esau, for stealing his birthright. As he wrestled in prayer with God for the answer, God allowed Jacob's angel to manifest himself, and there Jacob had an experience with this angel that not only assuaged his fears but changed his name and his nature and caused him to become a great man of Israel. His encounter, seeing the ladder with the angels ascending and descending and meeting him at God's camp, sets forth clear teaching that God's people, from the very beginning, have access to this wonderful angelic ministry.

On the other hand, failure is apparent as we study the account of Lot's wife in Genesis 19. Lot, the husband and priest of his home, must take his share of this failure. He chose to live with his family among evil men in the very depraved city of Sodom. There he vexed his righteous soul as described in the Bible. God must judge sin. Certainly, He must judge vile sin that leads men and women to change the use of the body against nature, as God created it. Men leave women and lust for other men, and women leave men to lust after other women. This sin comes under judgment.

God sends two of His faithful angels to rescue Lot's family and warns Lot to get the word to his children and leave Sodom quickly. This story is so well known by Bible readers that I will only dwell on the portion that deals with Lot's wife.

The angels, as they left Sodom, warned Lot's family, "Do not look back!" For some unexplained reason, Lot's wife turned to look back and immediately was transformed into a pillar of salt. It is very interesting that not only did the angel fail to rescue her from this fate, but Jesus, in speaking of His coming again said, **Remember Lot's wife** (Luke 17:32).

How infamous do you want to become? Would you have wanted the Lord Jesus to mention you publicly then have it recorded so that millions upon millions of readers down through the centuries would know of your failure?

Why did Jesus mention her? Certainly, it was not to bring shame to the memory of her. He had a greater motive than that. He mentioned her in the context of warning His people to avoid getting so carried away with eating, drinking, buying, selling, planting, reaping, building, and all of the consuming activities of a busy life, that the more important issues of eternity are neglected!

If we are looking in the Word of God for what turns our angel off and deactivates him in his ministry to and for us, we certainly have great insight here. In the context of His judgment coming on the world, Jesus warns of that which will cause us to miss deliverance. Noah and his family were saved. Lot and his daughters were saved even though his wife was lost. Notice the things Jesus mentioned in Luke 17:28 that can stop the deliverance of His saints, both now and in the end times.

1. They were filled with the lust of food and sex.

2. They **bought** and were carried away with buying and selling.

3. They sold and were given over to the amassing of profit.

4. They **builded** for the sake of pride and fortune. The warnings are all directly concerned with greed for wealth and abundance which is birthed out of pride and self-interest.

Jesus then said, **Whosoever shall seek to save his life shall lose it; and whosoever shall lose his life shall preserve it** (Luke 17:33). **To seek to save** [our] **life** simply means that we refuse to be embarrassed by a lack of worldly possessions, to the extent that we set out to get them by any and every means. The Word of God makes it clear that if we would seek first His kingdom, then all we have need of would be supplied. (Matt. 6:33.) Jesus is not referring to our *needs*, but our *greed*.

Was it greed, pride, or selfishness that made Lot's wife turn back toward the city and sacrifice her eternity with God? Lot and his two young daughters needed her desperately. The sordidness of sin in the lives of Lot and his two daughters from that time on is chronicled and well known.

Angels cannot successfully carry out their ministry of deliverance if we are given to the five things aforementioned in this chapter.

Another illustration of what greed can do to us and how it stops the ministering angel sent from God on our behalf can be found in Numbers 22-24.

In the beginning, Balaam was a great prophet in the land. Even the heathen kings knew of his great reputation. What he cursed would be cursed and what he blessed would be blessed. King Balak saw God's blessing on Israel and sought to have the prophet Balaam curse them. There is not sufficient space in this book to give a detailed account of Balaam's sin, but we will give a brief sketch.

God sent an angel to try and save Balaam from the error of his greed. The account is very humorous in that Balaam's mount was more spiritual than Balaam! He saw the angel

71

with the flashing sword, and Balaam didn't! Balaam must have been riding along preoccupied with one thing, the money that the wicked king had promised him. The donkey, being able to see the flashing sword in the hand of the angel, probably saved the prophet's life when he jumped around to avoid the sword. His life was saved in this experience, but apparently his soul was not. Revelation 2:14 reveals his sin.

If he had not been so greedy, loved God and appreciated the angel being sent to save him, perhaps he would have turned to join Israel, God's people, and would be in heaven today. Again, the attempt of God, through an angel, failed because this man was too caught up with worldly-mindedness. He could not receive the ministry of an angel sent from heaven to deliver him.

In the account of the rich man and Lazarus, the love of money stopped the ministry of angels. Lazarus, the poor beggar, literally died at the gate of the wealthy man. No doubt you could say that he died of starvation because the rich man ignored him and did not share his great wealth with one who needed it.

When Lazarus died, Luke 16:22 records that the angels carried him into the bliss of Abraham's bosom. The rich man also died, but there were no angels to carry him to the same place. If there is not a good angel assigned to attend your death and you have been too busy with the affairs of this life, then you have left yourself open to the same experience that the rich man had. He opened his eyes in hell and suffered torment forever. Hold on to the material things of this life lightly. Be ever ready at any time to freely, without any pain of surrender, give them up if God asks you!

One more Bible illustration of a man's failure can be found in Acts 12:7-11. Israel's King Herod seized Peter and put him in prison. He had perfect knowledge of God's blessing upon the disciples. He knew that Peter was miraculously delivered from a prison that was guarded with such security that it was impossible for a man to be able to escape without supernatural help. Peter was handcuffed to two guards, and there were sixteen other guards posted to watch him. In spite of Herod's knowledge that Peter's deliverance from prison was supernatural and because of his concern about his own reputation, he had the guards killed. (vv. 18,19.) Now the course is set, and it leads downward.

Herod, in his speech that reeked with pride, took all of the glory and gave none to God. He was brought up in Jewish tradition and was not ignorant of the results of pride and vain glory. The angel of the Lord, who could have come to aid him, now smites him. There is no longer any supernatural protection. Satan moves in, as he is prone to do when we are out of God's will and His protection. There is a void now where trust and humility should have been, and Satan moves in to fill it. Herod's body is destroyed by worms, and he dies. (vv. 21-23.) There is no angel to usher him in to God's presence.

It seems, in the aforementioned illustrations of failure, where the ministry of heavenly, God-sent angels was cut off, that there is a common denominator.

What was it that caused Lot's wife to turn back? What caused the downfall of Balaam? What brought about the death of the Jewish king, Herod?

In seeking to save, they lost. In these three cases, it was pride, love of money, and love of the applause of men. It can happen for a myriad of reasons, and as a result, one can be deprived of the aid of God's ministering angels and ultimately lose his soul!

Watch the little foxes, the little temptations, that lead to evil. God's Word promises:

> **There hath no temptation taken you but such as is common to man: but God is faithful, who will not**

suffer you to be tempted above that ye are able; but will with the temptation also make a way of escape, that ye may be able to bear it.

1 Corinthians 10:13

There is no reward for godless living that is worth losing the ministry of God's heaven-sent, ministering angels and perhaps ultimately your own soul.

Angel Chronicles

This story comes out of Africa. The wife of the pastor of a church had gone shopping and unknowingly entered into an area where rioting had just broken out. Men surrounded her car, broke the windows, seized the car keys and threw them into the bushes. They dragged her out into the street and were ready to rape and kill her.

Suddenly, a large, terrifying man approached and said, "Let her alone." As the frightened men backed off, he picked the woman up, took her to her car, placed her in the driver's seat, handed her the keys and said, "Leave quickly." As she drove off, she looked back to thank him for rescuing her, but he was gone!

This is just another example of God's great army ready to serve us.

9

Angels:
Deliverers or Destroyers?

In Acts 12:1-23, we find two stories: one of Simon Peter and the delivering angel and one of King Herod and the destroying angel.

King Herod began his persecution of the church by killing James, John's brother. These executions were usually accomplished by severing the head from the body. This act of treachery and murder seemed to please the Jews, so the king proceeded to arrest the leading disciple, Simon Peter.

Acts 12:3 makes it very clear that Herod was going to do to Peter what he did to James, thinking it would be even more pleasing to the Jewish leaders to kill the leader of the new Christian sect.

No doubt the common people were beginning to believe Jesus was alive, and His disciples were indeed working miracles among the people. If Herod put an end to this vexing Jewish problem, it would, in his estimation, elevate him to even a stronger position of leadership, both with Caesar in Rome and with the Sanhedrin and leadership in Israel.

But Herod had to wait until the Passover was over before Peter could be killed, so he was put in irons and chained between two soldiers in a dark, dismal cell. A double guard stood by the doors and extreme care was taken so Peter would not escape. While this diabolical plan is proceeding, there is another plan being brought into play to foil Satan's plan.

> **And, behold, the angel of the Lord came upon him [Peter], and a light shined in the prison: and he smote Peter on the side, and raised him up, saying, Arise up quickly. And his chains fell off from his hands.**
>
> **And the angel said unto him, Gird thyself, and bind on thy sandals. And so he did. And he saith unto him, Cast thy garment about thee, and follow me.**
>
> **And he went out, and followed him; and wist not that it was true which was done by the angel; but thought he saw a vision.**
>
> **When they were past the first and second ward, they came unto the iron gate that leadeth unto the city; which opened to them of his own accord: and they went out, and passed on through one street; and forthwith the angel departed from him.**
>
> **And when Peter was come to himself, he said, Now I know of a surety, that the Lord hath sent his angel, and hath delivered me out of the hand of Herod, and from all the expectation of the people of the Jews.**
>
> **Acts 12:7-11**

The saints in Jerusalem were in constant, earnest prayer for Peter. Inasmuch as the Bible does not tell us how they were praying for Peter, we can only surmise what was happening. It has historically been said that they were praying for his release. But, if they were praying that God would deliver him, then why were they surprised when they found him standing at the door? If they were praying for his release and were not expecting a supernatural deliverance, which it would most certainly take, then they were not praying in faith.

Faith, in order for it to be faith, must believe and expect the answer then should rejoice over that answer before it is received. *To rejoice over an expected answer before you receive it, as you would rejoice after you get it, is indeed true faith!*

76

There is something else to be considered. They could have been fervently praying for Peter that his faith would not fail as it did before when he denied his Lord. Was it possible that the disciples were concerned that Peter had not yet really proven himself worthy to be the leader? After all, he was impetuous, headstrong and given to making hasty decisions. This was a time when great care must be exercised if they were to continue. This scene we see of the disciples seeking God earnestly in prayer is an example for us. It teaches us the great value of prayer, even when we do not know how to pray for every situation.

There is yet another angle to be considered. Each of us has an angel that was appointed by the Father and given to watch over us as a guardian and protector. (Heb. 1:14, Matt. 18:10.) This angel is given to us at birth, delegated by God the Father to watch over us and to see that at all times God's perfect will is being fulfilled in our lives.

While not, in any way, minimizing the value of intercession and the fact that Peter needed all the prayer he could get, it seems to be that his ministering angel was the reason that Peter had this supernatural deliverance.

This incident leads me to believe that we have not always thoroughly understood the ministry of angels. No one, to my knowledge, has ever stated or written anything other than that it was the instrument of prayer that brought the angels down to get Peter out of prison.

Do we believe that angels, beholding the face of God and being in constant touch with Him at all times (Matt. 18:10) can, because of delegated authority, act on their own? If we can, then we can simplify the whole question and clear the air of all mystery surrounding these awesome, beautiful creatures.

We can move one step higher in our appreciation of the angels' wonderful ministry. With more understanding, we can exercise more faith and expectancy concerning their ministry to us and for us.

The authority, power, knowledge, ability, and wisdom of angels cannot be seriously questioned. This account of the delivering angel sent to literally spring Peter from the escape-proof security system seems to settle all questions about their flexible and diverse abilities.

When the young girl, Rhoda, heard Peter knocking on the door, she recognized Peter's voice. She hurriedly went and told the others, but they did not believe her. After all, Peter was in prison! Apparently, they were not expecting God to deliver Peter supernaturally out of captivity in the middle of the night! They argued with her, suggesting that perhaps she had seen Peter's angel.

In ancient times, it was believed that angels took on the likeness of the ones they were assigned to watch over. Apparently, she could not make them understand that she had not seen him, only heard him. For whatever it is worth, Peter kept on knocking. Finally, someone opened the door, and to their utter astonishment, there stood Peter!

This account of Peter's experience with his delivering angel leads us to some very solid principles concerning God's special gift to us of ministering angels.

1. Angels know what is transpiring here on earth at all times.

2. They are available to assist us in carrying out God's will for His Church.

3. They can cause a deep spell or sleep on the enemy and overcome strategies.

4. Barriers, even bars of iron, are easy for them to overcome.

5. They have complete control over all the hindrances the enemy puts before us to hamper our progress.

6. They will only do for us what we cannot do for ourselves.

7. When they assist us, they expect us to obey their instructions.

8. According to Peter's experience, seeing an angel is like having a vision.

How many times in Scripture do we read how the enemy tries to not only destroy the work of the Lord, but also His servants! If God had allowed Peter to be killed, as was James, the infant church could easily have been completely destroyed. A very difficult question comes before us. Why was Peter delivered and James, as well as countless other martyrs throughout the church age, not? Let us consider some thoughts.

1. Martyrdom has always been a part of the life of the church.

2. Sometimes saints, such as Peter, have been supernaturally spared. The reason seems to be that, if the death of a certain saint would completely extinguish all hope of the saints, then God would send His angel as He did here for Peter. Read, also, the experience of the Apostle Paul when he was about to lose his life in a shipwreck. (Acts 27.)

3. We recognize that these deliverances were more for the benefit of the young church inasmuch as both Peter and Paul were to become martyrs when they were old.

4. While martyrdom whets the appetite of the enemy to continue his diabolical persecution, it also encourages the faith of the saints that know earth is only temporary. Heaven is home, and it is forever.

Inasmuch as we, as human beings, are created lower than the angels (Heb. 2:7), we must consider their relationship to us.

They have never experienced the frailty of flesh as we know it. Neither have they known the death unto life transition of the joy of salvation. Because of this, is it possible that they are many, many times disappointed in our failure to walk more in obedience and holiness?

Peter was, at this time in his life, walking in careful obedience to the Lord, and he was zealous for the work. This marvelous supernatural deliverance has been placed in the Book for us to learn from and consider.

May we ever be open to teaching that will cause us to walk in holiness and obedience to God. Our unbelief could very easily interfere in his assignment to us.

Take courage, for you do have an angel to watch over you, whatever prison you are in. No matter how hopelessly bound you may be, God and His mighty angels stand ready to set you free in heaven-wrought deliverance!

King Herod, on the other hand, was a very evil king. To take space to write about his corrupt behavior is not necessary. The effect of his sin and wickedness was far reaching, but he went too far when he touched the glory of God. He did this when he accepted the praise of the people, and they proclaimed his voice as the voice of a god, and not of a man (Acts 12:22). Immediately thereafter, he was struck by an angel of the Lord, was eaten of worms and died.

Adam Clarke's Commentary helps to shed some light on the subject when he writes concerning 1 Corinthians 10:10 which says, **Neither murmur ye, as some of them also murmured, and were destroyed of the destroyer.** His comments are as follows: ''The Jews suppose that God employed *destroying angels* to punish those rebellious Israelites; they were *five* in number, and one of them they call *Meshachith*, the destroyer; which appears to be another name for *Samael* the *angel of death* to whose influence they attribute all deaths which are not *uncommon* or *violent*.

Those who die violent deaths, or deaths that are not in the *common* manner of men, are considered as perishing by immediate judgments from God."[1]

Concerning 1 Corinthians 10:10, Moffat's translation states, **only to be destroyed by the destroying angel.** Beck's translation says, "the angel of death killed them."

Always remember that the Bible is so written that one can read it and come away with their own interpretation and understanding of the nature of God regarding certain issues.

Is death from heaven, or is it a result of the fall of man when Satan and his angels became the rulers of this age? Is disease, sickness, and suffering the will of God, as some teach? Or is it in earth's realm as the result of disobedience and sin?

It seems that, on this earth, death is everywhere. Accidents, disease, and catastrophes take multitudes everyday. What about singular deaths such as Herod's and the children of Israel when they rebelled in the wilderness?

Hebrews 2:14 attributes the power of death to Satan, but it also states that **through death he [Jesus] might destroy him that had the power of death, that is, the devil; And deliver them who through fear of death were all their lifetime subject to bondage.** In other words, Satan has the power of death, and God has the power of life. Death comes from Satan, but life comes from God.

The thief comes to steal, kill and destroy. (John 10:10.) Satan is that thief and has fallen angels that were cast out with him onto the earth. (Rev. 12:9.)

In this chapter, we have seen examples of angels that deliver and angels that destroy. Are these all the same angels, with different missions and assignments? Or are

---

[1]Adam Clarke, *The New Testament . . . With a Commentary and Critical Notes,* 3 vol. reprint ed. (Nashville: Abington, n.d.) 3:245.

there different ones? Are they the angels of God sent to kill and destroy? Or is it Satan and his angels that God allows, because of the faithlessness or rebellion of man, to be the killers and destroyers?

You have read here several different views of this subject. Each one of us must form our own opinion from all of the information that can be gathered.

It is my belief that God allows the fallen angels to be used for special punishment, or death, today even as He did in the Old Testament. Psalm 78:49 records when **He cast upon them the fierceness of his anger, wrath, and indignation, and trouble, by sending evil angels among them.** Death abides here on earth, not in heaven, and is allowed by God, in specific cases, to be overcome, along with sickness and disease, when a believer takes authoritative action. By using the powerful Name of our Lord Jesus in faith against Satan, Satan can only fail!

This same authority and power can also employ the assistance of angels to deliver us as they did Peter and multitudes unheralded down through the ages past.

I trust that you, as you read this book, will come to comprehend that it is up to you. Your will and your relationship with God will determine the outcome in every encounter and spiritual conflict that comes to you as a result of living in a sin cursed world.

Satan has come to steal, kill, and destroy, but Jesus came to give us abundant, overflowing, plentiful, rich, replete life. (John 10:10.)

Angel Chronicles

A pastor once related to me a story about his daughter who had moved to a very large city to find employment. One day her car broke down in the middle of a busy intersection, in one of the most crime ridden sections of that city. There was nothing to do but to leave her car in the intersection and go to a phone booth to call for help.

As she was phoning, she felt a tap on her shoulder and turned and saw a tall, nicely dressed man who said, ''You are in trouble, aren't you?'' When she said yes, he told her to follow him. She felt peace and walked out with him to her car.

His car was parked behind hers, his front bumper touching her rear bumper. He told her to get in and get ready to start it. He raised the hood of her car and adjusted something and told her to turn on the ignition. She did, and it started immediately. When she looked around to thank him, both he and his car were gone.

She believes, and I do too, that it was an angel.

10
Heaven's Observers

Paul, in 1 Corinthians 4:9, said that apostles were **made a spectacle unto the world, and to angels, and to men.** Jesus referred to angels as ascending and descending upon Him. (John 1:51.) Paraphrasing this you could say He was surrounded by them. Jesus also said that whosoever would confess Him before men would be confessed by the Son of Man before the angels of God. Conversely, those who deny Him would be denied before the angels of God. (Luke 12:8,9.)

Isn't it amazing that the Bible has been in print for 500 years, yet the church has virtually ignored the ministry of angels? They have relegated it to a children's realm where angels are perceived as heavenly beings who are sent to watch over us as children but who leave the scene after we grow up!

Very seldom does a minister or pastor teach about or refer to them. The Scriptures, however, not only teach us of their presence but also give us a warning about how we are to acknowledge their valuable ministry.

1. Angels are always present around us. (Ps. 34:7.)

2. Angels hear the Lord Jesus confess the names of those who are saved. (Luke 12:8.)

3. Angels rejoice over those who repent of their sins and come to the Lord. (Luke 15:10.)

4. Angels surrounded the Lord in such numbers that He could have had legions of them at His disposal. (Matt. 26:53.)

5. Angels came and ministered to Him at crucial times in His life. (Matt. 4:11, Luke 22:43.)

6. Angels are reapers. They, in the future, will cast out those that practice lawlessness. (Matt. 13:39-42.)

7. If we offend or despise a little one that believes in the Lord, the angels will take note of it. (Matt. 18:10.)

8. Angels that come back with Jesus at His return will take notice of those who were ashamed of Him. (Mark 8:38.)

9. Angels are present at the death of saints and escort them into Heaven. (Luke 16:22.)

10. Angels guarded the body of Jesus in the tomb. (John 20:12.)

11. Angels are ministering spirits. (Heb. 1:14.)

12. Angels are worshippers of God. (Heb. 1:6.)

13. We have sometimes entertained angels without being aware of it. (Heb. 13:2.)

14. Angels desire to look into or understand our redemption and salvation. (1 Peter 1:12.)

This is a mere skimming of the surface of the myriad of Scriptures that allude to the ministry of these majestic, beautiful, created beings.

It is clearly taught throughout Scriptures that not only are angels present on this earth carrying out the directives of God, but that we are also to be aware of them. The warning of the Lord Jesus to us is that we acknowledge their existence and respect their functions.

Constantly and consistently throughout all of Scripture, the presence of angels is taught as being involved in the affairs of man. They are here. They encamp around about us. They have been given charge over us. They bear us up. They confess us before our heavenly Father, and they listen to the words that we speak.

In Ecclesiastes, we find an admonition to:

> **Suffer not thy mouth to cause thy flesh to sin; neither say thou before the angel, that it was an error: wherefore should God be angry at thy voice, and destroy the work of thine hands?**
>
> **Ecclesiastes 5:6**

What a warning to us to watch the words of our mouth! When we speak, we speak before our angel. Inasmuch as the Bible does not teach us in this text what the wrong thing to say is, we must go to other Scripture to learn the correct use of the tongue.

Various translations of Matthew 12:36,37 express the importance of what we say before our angel. These verses teach us that we shall be judged for every idle, thoughtless, careless word, and by our words we will either be justified or condemned. What a severe warning our Lord Jesus gives concerning idle, non-working words! This is supported by other verses, especially the book of James.

If only our eyes could be opened to see our guardian angels as they stand by us! If we could watch them intently, we would see their expression change as idle, careless, faithless words fall from our lips. Surely we would be more careful if we could see them, but God has ordained that we walk by faith and not by sight. We are to simply be obedient to His Word.

Proverbs speaks of the power of pleasant or suitable words. This same book also speaks of the power of the tongue. The word *power* comes from the Hebrew word *yad* which signifies an "open hand" as opposed to a "closed hand." In light of this, the Scripture from Proverbs 18:21 that says, **Death and life are in the *power* of the tongue** could determine whether or not one will have eternal, physical death or everlasting life in heaven.

In James 1:6, we are warned against wavering after we have asked for something from the Lord. This is a principle of faith. If we ask and then waver, we are not to expect anything from the Lord. Thus the tongue, not rightly used, can wipe out our prayer and faith. The truth expressed in James 1:26 teaches me that if we do not bridle or control our tongue but allow it to contradict our believing heart, then our efforts before the Lord are useless.

It is difficult to understand why so many men in the ministry find fault with the preaching that calls attention to the power of our words or, as it is so often called, the confession of the Word. It is the very crux of the text of this book. We are warned very pointedly to watch our words, what we confess before our angel, lest God destroy our efforts.

There are definite warnings about the words that can deactivate your angel and render his ministry ineffective: a lifestyle of negative conversation that includes gossip, condemnation, and judgment, words that discourage or maybe even destroy another saint, words that would wound instead of heal, words of dissension in the church, words of doubt, wavering and fear that cultivate unbelief.

Your angel already knows about the finished work of the cross and how Jesus our Lord took our sins and our diseases there to pay a terrible price. When we speak any words that detract from or minimize that finished work, there is no doubt that we dismay our angel and discourage the angel's ministry in our behalf.

I recall being with a pastor who poured out all of his difficulties to me and ended by saying, "I just don't know what I am going to do." I did empathize with him in his situation, but I asked him if he believed that God could help him with his problem? He quickly responded, "Yes." "But," I said, "You didn't say that. You said you didn't know what you were going to do!" Immediately he saw what he was doing and corrected his speech. I wanted him to realize that his words had the power to help or to hinder.

What a big difference our words make! They can change the very atmosphere around us. If it is possible for us to deactivate our angels by our doubting words, then it is also possible that evil angels can move in, fill the void, and make our situation worse than it was before.

Jesus taught in Luke 12:8,9 that if we deny Him before men, He will deny us before the angels. What happens when, by our idle and careless words, we deny His power and ability to work in our behalf? Is that not the same as denying the Lord before His angels? Is that not saying the wrong thing before our angel?

Any kind of denial by our words of God's power is not only unbelief, but sin, and is heard loudly in the heavens. We are denying His ability, power, compassion, and willingness before all.

Sometimes an emotional response from us concerning a Christian friend who is experiencing the trying of his faith can be idle words.

They are words born of sympathy on our part, but they do not encourage the hurting saint. May God give us the wisdom to empathize but, at the same time, speak words of life and encouragement. We believe that angels are sent to minister to those who are heirs of salvation. Let us strive to speak words that will invoke their help in behalf of the troubled saint instead of ignoring their powerful presence!

It is possible to express love and compassion and still lift up a hurting brother or sister with words of hope and encouragement from the Scriptures. Please be very careful to watch what you say in every situation.

There are so many good words that we can speak. Words of health, faith-building words, and pleasant, kind words will lift people up instead of discouraging them. While we cannot carry another saint by our faith, it is possible to either help or hinder by our conversation.

Angel Chronicles

Dr. Glenn Burris Sr., Southeast District Supervisor for the Foursquare Church International, shared this story with me.

He and his wife had retired for the night. He was awakened about 3:00 a.m. by a voice that said, ''Your house is on fire.'' He thought it was only a dream. Since he did not smell smoke, he went back to sleep.

The voice again awakened him, repeating the warning. Again he did not smell smoke or sense anything was wrong, so he went back to sleep.

The third time the voice said, ''Your house is on fire, and this is the last time I am warning you!'' This time he opened the door to the living room, and a sheet of flames rushed toward him. It was his habit to leave the garden hose on the opposite side of the house, but this time he had left it near the door. So he seized the garden hose and was able to put out the flames.

Through this experience, he learned to recognize the voice of his angel and act at his command!

11
Angels and Healing

Do angels have anything to do with the healing of the sick? If evil angels can make man sick unto death as was the case with King Herod, then to believe that good angels can bring healing to the physical body is not amiss either. Let us consider the account of the sick man at the pool of Bethesda:

> Now there is at Jerusalem by the sheep market a pool, which is called in the Hebrew tongue Bethesda, having five porches. In these lay a great multitude of impotent folk, of blind, halt, withered, waiting for the moving of the water. For an angel went down at a certain season into the pool, and troubled the water: whosoever then first after the troubling of the water stepped in was made whole of whatsoever disease he had.
>
> And a certain man was there, which had an infirmity thirty and eight years.
>
> When Jesus saw him lie, and knew that he had been now a long time in that case, he saith unto him, Wilt thou be made whole?
>
> The impotent man answered him, Sir, I have no man, when the water is troubled, to put me into the pool: but while I am coming, another steppeth down before me.
>
> Jesus saith unto him, Rise, take up thy bed, and walk. And immediately the man was made whole, and took up his bed, and walked: and on the same day was the sabbath.
>
> **John 5:2-9**

This account of the sick man at the pool of Bethesda can be used to support that the *King James* Bible is from the manuscripts that many believe were not tampered with, even though there were manuscripts earlier that were later used for modern translations. So many other translations omit verses three and four in their works, saying that these are not adequately supported by the original manuscripts.

Some even contend that if this is a true account, then why did not the other writers of the New Testament mention it? This is not difficult to understand inasmuch as it is generally accepted that not all healings and events were recorded by all of the writers of the gospels.

Let us examine this account so accurately reported by the writer, John. First of all, there must have been such a place as the pool of Bethesda or John would not have had anything to record. It must have been a place where so many sick were gathered together that John describes them as a great multitude of those who are impotent, blind, halt, and withered.

Even today visitors in Jerusalem are shown the ruins of such a pool. It is inconceivable that a great multitude of sick people would gather at such a place if nothing had ever happened there before. There must have been an incentive for them, in their suffering, to come in all kinds of weather.

Now, let us turn our attention to the Lord Jesus. He certainly did visit these poor, sick, impotent people. He, our compassionate Lord Jesus, not only visited this place but worked one of His healing miracles there. It is interesting to note that He worked this miracle on the suffering man who had been there the longest.

Our focus in this chapter has been to endeavor to ascertain whether or not angels are used by God to minister divine healing. We cannot ignore certain truths that support this theory. Along with considering what Jesus chose to say, we must also consider what He chose not to say, being careful of course not to read into what has already been recorded. Note for example that Jesus did not grow angry at the man for thinking that he could receive healing by being there in that particular place. Nor is it recorded that Jesus preached a sermon to the sick who were there. He did not call them deluded or imply that they were wasting their time being there.

Would our Lord Jesus, knowing that history would record all, want the world to think that he supported such a place if it were not true that an angel did, at a certain time, trouble the water so that the first individual to enter the pool would receive healing? I do not believe so, and I think most people would agree.

The Bible does not say that the angel healed anyone, but it does say that he would trouble the water. Seeing that the angel did not bring healing, he did something to the water to cause the first one in to be healed. Many could say, "Maybe it was the faith of the person, not the water or the angel that brought healing." While faith in God is necessary, the account does not support any reasoning that ignores the appearance of the angel at a certain time to trouble the water.

Let us assume that angels can be used of God to minister, in some way, physical healing to God's people. If we can accept and believe that angels are messengers sent to minister to and for the heirs of salvation as stated in Hebrews 1:14, then can we include healing as part of that ministry?

I, for one, would rather miss it on the positive side and believe that God does use angels to help us in every way, including healing, than to have a closed mind and miss it completely.

If we can pray and say, "Lord, please allow your angels to protect us on this trip" then would we be so wrong to say, "Send your angel to minister to us in this time of physical need?"

You are free to make up your own mind on the subject. God's Word does record this great incident. It does mention that the angel was involved. We would not be out of line to believe that God can do the same today.

What is one conclusion we can be very safe in assuming? God is a very merciful, kind, and compassionate Heavenly Father. His attitude towards us is, "I want my children to be happy. I want my children to be free from Satan's attack of diabolical diseases. I want my children to enjoy the abundant life. I want my children to receive all of the finished work of the cross. I want my children to be free from all of the curses brought on the human race by Adam's fall. I want my children to enjoy all of the benefits paid for at the cross by the second Adam. I do not want the horrible death of my Son to have been suffered in vain. I do not want my people to only receive half of the benefit of the cross in salvation, but I also want them to be in health." As His Word declares, **Beloved, I wish above all things that thou mayest prosper and be in health, even as thy soul prospereth** (3 John 2).

W. E. Vine brings out that the Greek word for "prosper" is *euodoo*. In the passive voice and present tense this word "suggests the successive circumstances of varying prosperity as week follows week"[1] in the prosperity of physical and spiritual health.

This is God's attitude toward His children. All heaven has been made available to us, including His mighty angels. Let us so believe, that we will be open to receive! Stay in steadfast obedience and holiness and keep a smile on your angel's face!

---

[1]W. E. Vine, *An Expository Dictionary of New Testament Words* (Old Tappan, New Jersey: Fleming H. Revell, 1966), p. 225.

Angel Chronicles

The following account was told to me concerning a family that was called to the hospital following a terrible automobile wreck involving a loved one.

The family was led into the hospital room and told that there was no hope. The doctor left, and as they stood around the bed praying, the eyes of one of the family members were opened, and he saw a large angel enter the room and lay both of his hands on the patient's face. The doctor returned. He immediately noticed a change and said that perhaps, after all, there was some hope.

He left the room and again they prayed. Again, the angel appeared and repeated his action. When the doctor came in this time, he marvelled at what he saw. The severely injured man fully recovered, and the family is still thankful and gives praise to God for sending an angel in their time of need.

Angel Chronicles

In 2 Samuel 12:14-23, King David's baby was sick unto death. Verses 22 and 23 contain David's great statement that has, through the years, encouraged so many parents who have lost a child, **I shall go to him, but he shall not return to me.**

May this angel chronicle be a blessing to those who have lost little ones in death. Dr. Kenneth E. Hagin relates this beautiful story.

A couple he knew had lost their beautiful little child in death. As everyone would, they had a most difficult time. One evening, as they were sitting in their home lost in grief, a knock came at the door. Opening it, they found a stranger who walked past them, entered the room and began to talk to them in a very beautiful way about their child. He said the child was with Jesus and that they should not continue to weep. Then the stranger got up and walked into the bedroom that belonged to the child. He began to take clothing from the closet and pile it on the floor saying, ''You must take these things and give them to a child who needs them,'' and then he turned the little child's picture face down and said, as he walked to the door, ''You must get on with your lives, serve Jesus, and mourn no more.'' At this, the mother and father felt great peace and walked out to express how thankful they were for these words of hope, but the stranger had disappeared.

If you have lost a son or daughter, believe that this same beautiful message belongs to you.

Angel Chronicles

Pastor Don Duncan of New Braunfels, Texas, shares this story. As an officer in Vietnam during battle, the Lord had spared his life many times, but this chronicle is outstanding.

He was sitting at his desk working at the many details for which an officer is responsible when his pencil rolled off of his desk. As he bent down and reached for his pencil, a soldier who had gone berserk under the stress of battle burst through the door with his gun firing right at the spot where, a moment before, Don had been sitting. Had he not, at that precise moment, bent down to pick up the pencil, his body would have been riddled with bullets. Someone nudged that pencil so that it rolled off the desk!

A thousand shall fall at thy side, and then thousand at thy right hand; but it shall not come nigh thee. For He shall give his angels charge over thee, to keep thee in all thy ways.

Psalm 91:7,11

Conclusion

For there stood by me this night the angel of God whose I am and whom I serve, saying, fear not, Paul; thou must be brought before Caesar, and lo, God hath given thee all them that sail with thee.

Acts 27:23,24

This story of deliverance of both Paul and the entire ship of 276 souls furnishes a fitting conclusion to the activity of angels.

1. Only those who know the Lord Jesus, or will come to know Him, receive their ministry.

2. Those who serve their God will receive very specific details of impending danger.

3. Angels deal in specific details such as, if the soldiers had fled the ship as they tried to do, then the others would not be spared.

4. In the presence of angels, you will not only receive ministry but great peace and joy in the midst of severe trials.

5. Deliverance by angels should lead to the conversion of others, as it did with the people on board the ship.

If you have never received Jesus Christ, God's Son, as your personal Savior, do so today. Without a relationship with God and His holy angels through Jesus Christ, you are not covered, and you're left to, as the world expresses it, trust in luck only.

Good angels as well as evil angels encamp around us. You are receiving the benefit of either the good or the evil. You will be the one to make the choice. Make the right one and have peace, protection, and great joy the rest of your life!

Remember these words: Angels are greater in power and might. (2 Peter 2:11.)

References

Scripture quotations marked ASV are taken from the *American Standard Version*. Copyright © 1901 by Thomas Nelson & Sons and copyright © 1929 by International Council of Religious Education.

Scripture quotations marked AMP are taken from *The Amplified Bible, New Testament*. Copyright © 1958, 1987 by the Lockman Foundation, La Habra, California. Used by permission.

Some Scripture quotations are taken from *The Bible. A New Translation*. Copyright © 1950, 1952, 1953, 1954 by James A. R. Moffat, Harper & Row Publishers, Inc. New York, New York.

Scripture quotations marked NIV are taken from *The Holy Bible: New International Version*. Copyright © 1973, 1978, 1984 by the International Bible Society. Used by permission of Zondervan Bible Publishers.

Some Scripture quotations marked NKJV are taken from *The New King James Version of the Bible*. Copyright © 1979, 1980, 1982 by Thomas Nelson, Inc., Publishers. Used by permission.

Some Scripture quotations are taken from *The Holy Bible in the Language of Today: an American Translation* by William F. Beck. Copyright © 1976 William F. Beck and A. J. Holman Co. (division of J. B. Lippincott Co.), Philadelphia and New York.

Roy H. Hicks is a successful minister of the Gospel who together with his wife Margaret has given his life to pastoring and pioneering churches throughout the United States. He has served the Lord in various foreign fields, having made missionary journeys to South America, the Orient, Australia, and New Zealand.

As a dedicated man of God, Dr. Hicks formerly served as General Supervisor of the Foursquare Gospel Church and has become a popular speaker at charismatic conferences and churches.

Perhaps the thing that most endears Dr. Hicks to readers is his warmth and his ability to reach out as the true believer he is — a man of strong, positive faith, sharing a refreshing ministry through the power and anointing of the Holy Spirit.

To contact Dr. Hicks
write:
Dr. Roy H. Hicks
P. O. Box 4113
San Marcos, California 92069

*Please include your prayer requests
and comments when you write.*

Other Books by Dr. Roy H. Hicks

Obtaining Bible Promises
A Different Approach for Every Promise

Keys of the Kingdom

Instrument-Rated Christian

Healing Your Insecurities

Praying Beyond God's Ability
Why Prayers Go Unanswered

Use It or Lose It
The Word of Faith

He Who Laughs Lasts and Lasts and Lasts

Another Look at the Rapture

The Power of Positive Resistance
The Christian's Antihistamine

Final Days and Counting

Whatever Happened to Hope?

**Available from your local bookstore
or by writing:**

Harrison House
P. O. Box 35035
Tulsa, OK 74153

In Canada contact:

Word Alive
P. O. Box 284
Niverville, Manitoba
CANADA R0A 1E0

For international sales in Europe,
contact:

Harrison House Europe
Belruptstrasse 42 A
A — 6900 Bregenz
AUSTRIA

The Harrison House Vision

Proclaiming the truth and the power
Of the Gospel of Jesus Christ
With excellence;

Challenging Christians to
Live victoriously,
Grow spiritually,
Know God intimately.